ANTHROPOLOGICAL PAPERS
MUSEUM OF ANTHROPOLOGY, UNIVERSITY OF MICHIGAN
NO. 22

# BIBLIOGRAPHY OF MICHIGAN ARCHAEOLOGY

by
ALEXIS A. PRAUS

ANN ARBOR
THE UNIVERSITY OF MICHIGAN, 1964

ISBN (print): 978-1-949098-23-5
ISBN (ebook): 978-1-949098-71-6

Browse all of our books at
sites.lsa.umich.edu/archaeology-books.

Order our books from the University of Michigan
Press at www.press.umich.edu.

For permissions, questions, or manuscript queries,
contact Museum publications by email at umma-pubs@umich.edu or visit the Museum website at
lsa.umich.edu/ummaa.

# FOREWORD

This is the first bibliography of Michigan archaeology compiled since Harlan I. Smith published his *Memoranda Towards a Bilbliography of the Archaeology of Michigan* in 1912. Much has been written since and it is hoped that this compilation will be of value to both the professional and to the amateur. Many of the entries will not be of interest or use to the contemporary archaeologist. Though they may not be important from the scientific standpoint, they will, however, be of value to the student of the history of archaeology in Michigan.

With this in mind, all references to Michigan archaeology have been included with the exception of those to be found in newspapers, atlases, and most county histories. Some of the minor references cited call attention to sites, artifacts, and archaeological features otherwise not available in one volume to the archaeologist, historian, or geographer.

Like all similar works, this publication is the sum of the efforts of many people and many organizations. The staffs of all libraries used proved true to their dedication to service and assistance to the researcher. Many extended courtesies well beyond those expected of them. The collections of Michigan public libraries represented in this bibliography are those of Detroit, Grand Rapids, and Kalamazoo. The University of Michigan and Michigan State University libraries are important repositories of printed archaeological information that is available to all, as it was to the compiler. Such libraries as the Boston Public Library and those of the Chicago Natural History Museum, Harvard Peabody Museum, and the State Historical Society of Wisconsin kindly sent necessary books on interlibrary loan. Special and personal thanks are due to Mrs. Esther Loughin of the Michigan State Library at Lansing. Her personal, as well as professional, interest in this bibliography is fully appreciated. Both the Chicago Public Library and the Newberry Library contain many archaeological references in their large holdings. Many are represented in this publication. The Library of the Royal Ontario Museum, Toronto, Canada, made books available from its collections via the mails – a good example of the international flow of information. It is not possible to thank, here, all of the individuals who helped in this compilation. The following, however, must receive acknowledgment: Homer L. Burch, Grand Rapids; Ira Butterfield, Bay City; the late Newell Collins; Harvey Franz,

Benton Harbor; Kenneth Kidd, Toronto, Canada, and Carl Parchert, Dearborn. Miss Howard, Curator of Education at the Kalamazoo Public Museum, helped in all phases and was specially valuable in checking and proofreading.

Dr. J. B. Griffin of the University of Michigan encouraged and urged the preparation of this bibliography and was especially helpful in suggesting its final form and content.

Entries in the bibliography are arranged alphabetically and are numbered consecutively. Each author's contribution is, in turn, listed chronologically. Annotations have been added if the contents of an entry were not obvious from the title. No attempt has been made to evaluate references cited. Their inclusion is indicative of their presumed value.

The brief index included, it is hoped, will make the bibliography easier to use.

No bibliography is ever complete and this one is no exception. Accuracy was conscientiously strived for, though certainly not achieved.

Any errors and omissions brought to the attention of the compiler, will be noted, filed, and perhaps made available to the public at a later date.

Alexis A. Praus

# BIBLIOGRAPHY OF MICHIGAN ARCHAEOLOGY

## A

1. Abbott, Charles C. Primitive Industry: Or Illustrations of the Handiwork, in Stone, Bone, and Clay, of the Native Races of the Northern Atlantic Seaboard of America. Salem, Mass., George A. Bates, 1881, vi + 560 pp. Illus.

Quote of Henry Gillman's description of a Michigan birdstone and his statement of the use of birdstones p. 370. Taken from entry No. 241.

2. Adam, John J. Lenawee County: Early History of Lenawee County. *In:* Michigan Pioneer and Historical Collections, Vol. II. Detroit, William Graham's Presses, 1880, pp. 357-387.

Records a peculiar earthwork on north bank of Raisin River in the northeast part of the village (now city) of Tecumseh.

3. The American Antiquarian, Vol. I, No. 1. Chicago, Jameson and Morse, April, 1878, p. 52.

Brief statement about the Indian artifacts possessed by the Detroit Academy of Science, including perforated skulls and other skeletal material in charge of Bela Hubbard.

4. Ancient Garden Beds of Michigan. Michigan History Magazine, Vol. XXVII, Winter No. Michigan Historical Commission, Lansing, 1943, pp. 673-684, 8 illus.

5. The Antiquarian, Vol. I, Pt. 12. Columbus, O., The Landon Printing and Publishing Co., Dec., 1897, p. 333.

Short statement about the Charles W. Manktelow collection of Indian artifacts, Cadillac, Michigan.

6. Appy, E. P. Ancient Mining in America. The American Antiquarian and Oriental Journal, Vol. XI, No. 2. Mendon, Ill., S. D. Peet, March, 1889, pp. 92-99.

A general article on ancient mining quoting Jacob Houghton on copper mining in the Lake Superior region. See entry No. 350.

7. The "Argillite" Culture of Michigan. Michigan Archaeological Society News, Vol. I, No. 1. Michigan Archaeological Society, Ann Arbor, Jan., 1953, pp. 3-4, 1 illus.

Describes argillite points in the University of Michigan Museum collections from various sites.

## B

8. Baggerly, Carmen. Waterworn and Glaciated Stone Tools from the Thumb District of Michigan. American Antiquity, Vol. XX, No. 2. The Society for American Archaeology, Salt Lake City, Utah, 1954, pp. 171-173.

Description of several thousand stone tools found near Imlay City. Some doubt if man-made.

9. Baker, R. Ray. Michigan's Mound Builders. Michigan History, Vol. XXIX, No. 3. Michigan Historical Commission, Lansing, July-Sept., 1945, pp. 313-318, 1 illus.

A general account of Michigan mounds.

10. Barrett, S. A. Aboriginal Copper Mines at McCargoe's Cove, Isle Royal [sic]. Yearbook of the Public Museum of the City of Milwaukee, Vol. IV. Milwaukee Public Museum, Milwaukee, Wis., Oct., 1926, pp. 20-36, 12 illus. 4 maps.

11. Bartol, Fred. Ball Banners. Ohio Archaeologist, N.S., Vol. I, No. 2. Ohio Indian Relic Collectors Society, Columbus, July, 1951, pp. 20-22, 2 illus.

Illustrates three Michigan ball banners.

12. Baum, Henry Mason, and Frederick Bennett Wright, editors. Prehistoric Remains in Michigan. Records of the Past, Vol. III. Records of the Past Exploration Society, Washington, D. C., 1904, pp. 95-96, 1 illus.

Contains an illustration of Bronson Park Mound, Kalamazoo, Michigan.

13. Baxter, Albert. History of the City of Grand Rapids, Michigan. New York and Grand Rapids, Munsell and Co., 1891. Chap. 1, "Location and Surroundings," pp. 1-21; Section, "Archaeology," pp. 14-19, 2 illus.

14. Bayport Chert. The Totem Pole, Vol. XI, No. 6. Aboriginal Research Club, Detroit, Mich., Sept., 1943, pp. 1-5.

Extracts from entry No. 122.

15. Bennett, Agnes Spaulding. Moccasin Bluff. The Totem Pole, Vol. XXXII, No. 2. Aboriginal Research Club, Detroit, Mich., May, 1953, pp. 1-6.

16. ——. Moccasin Bluff. The Totem Pole, Vol. XXXII, No. 3. Aboriginal Research Club, Detroit, Mich., June, 1953, p. 1.

A summary of cultures found at Moccasin Bluff.

17. Bettarel, Robert, and Sidney Harrison. An Early Ossuary in Michigan. Michigan Archaeologist, Vol. VIII, No. 4. Michigan Archaeological Society, Ann Arbor, Dec., 1962, pp. 37-42, 3 illus.

18. Binford, Lewis R. The Haltiner Copper Cache. Michigan Archaeologist, Vol. VII, No. 2. Michigan Archaeological Society, Ann Arbor, June, 1961, pp. 8-10, 1 illus.

19. Blois, John T. Gazetteer of the State of Michigan. Detroit, Sydney L. Rood and Co., 1838.

The origin of archaeological remains discussed on pages 161-177; describes and locates mounds, forts and garden beds; tells of Blois opening the Springwells Township mounds in 1837 and gives their contents. Earliest archaeological work in Michigan.

20. ——. Excavation of a Burial Mound Near Fort Wayne, Detroit. Michigan Archaeologist, Vol. IV, No. 4. Michigan Archaeological Society, Ann Arbor, Dec., 1958, pp. 73-75.

Extract from entry No. 19, pp. 168-173.

21. Bonner, Richard Illenden, editor. Memoirs of Lenawee County, Michigan. Western Historical Association, Madison, Wis., 1909, Vol. I, Chap. 1, "Lenawee County Antiquities," pp. 17-30.

22. Books and Maps. Michigan Archaeological Society News, Vol. II, No. 1, Michigan Archaeological Society, Ann Arbor, Jan., 1955, p. 6, 1 map.

Includes a map of rivers that can be used in conjunction with proposed system for site recording. See entry No. 43.

23. Borener, Fred. Brills Lake Site, Jackson County, Michigan. The Totem Pole, Vol. XLIII, No. 9. Aboriginal Research Club, Detroit, Mich., Dec., 1960, 6 unnumbered pp., 5 illus.

24. Boudeman, Donald O. Bird-Stone Ceremonial Found on Skull. The Wisconsin Archeologist, N.S., Vol. XXIV, No. 2. Wisconsin Archeological Society, Milwaukee, 1943, pp. 17-20, 1 illus.

Indian skeleton found in Wakeshma Township, Kalamazoo County, in sitting position with a slate birdstone on its skull. Three shell gorgets also found.

25. Brees, Perry. Bevelled Spears. The Totem Pole, Vol. IV, No. 3. Aboriginal Research Club, Detroit, Mich., Dec. 1939, p. 3.

Calls attention to the characteristics of beveled spears, especially the notch.

26. Brown, Charles E. The Stone Spud. The Wisconsin Archeologist [O. S.], Vol. II, No. 1. Archeological Section of the Wisconsin Natural History Society, Milwaukee, Oct., 1902, pp. 15-28.

Mention of spud-shaped copper implements from Ontonagon, Michigan, page 23.

27. ——. The Native Copper Implements of Wisconsin. The Wisconsin Archeologist [O.S.], Vol. III, No. 2. Wisconsin Archeological Society, Milwaukee, Jan., 1904, pp. 49-84, 15 illus.

Prehistoric Lake Superior copper mines; methods of mining, and special types of copper artifacts found in Michigan, pp. 54-55.

28. ——. The Native Copper Ornaments of Wisconsin. The Wisconsin Archeologist [O.S.], Vol. III, No. 3. Wisconsin Archeological Society, Milwaukee, April, 1904, pp. 101-121, 10 illus.

Miscellaneous references to copper artifacts from Michigan.

29. ——. Barbed Stone Axes. The Wisconsin Archeologist, N.S., Vol. IX, No. 3. Wisconsin Archeological Society, Milwaukee, April, 1930, pp. 139-143, 1 illus.

Michigan barbed axes, their description and distribution. Also describes some private collections and their contents.

30. ——. Additional Barbed Stone Axes. The Wisconsin Archeologist, N.S., Vol. XVIII, No. 2. Wisconsin Archeological Society, Milwaukee, Jan., 1938, pp. 63-64.

Same as above.

31. Brown, C[harles] E., and M. F. Hulburt. Some Village and Camp Sites in Northern Michigan. The Wisconsin Archeologist, N.S., Vol. IX, No. 4. Wisconsin Archeological Society, Milwaukee, July, 1930, pp. 180-184.

32. Brown, Theo. T. The Largest Copper Knives. The Wisconsin Archeologist, N.S., Vol. IX, No. 3. Wisconsin Archeological Society, Milwaukee, April, 1930, pp. 145-146.

A thirteen and seven-eighths-inch-long Michigan copper knife described, as well as some from Wisconsin.

33. Burch, Homer L. [editor]. [no title]. The Coffinberry News-Bulletin, Vol. III, No. 2. Wright L. Coffinberry Chapter, Michigan Archaeological Society, Grand Rapids, Feb., 1956. 4 unnumbered pp., 3 illus.

Reprint of articles from "Chips from the Totem Pole." See entries No. 633, 634, 635.

34. ——. [editor]. The Michigan Axe. The Coffinberry News-Bulletin, Vol. III, No. 5. Wright L. Coffinberry Chapter, Michigan Archaeological Society, Grand Rapids, May, 1956, pp. 2-3, 1 illus.

Includes illustration of three Kent County grooved axes.

35. ——. [editor]. [no title]. The Coffinberry News-Bulletin, Vol. III, No. 9. Wright L. Coffinberry Chapter, Michigan Archaeological Society, Grand Rapids, Nov., 1956, pp. 2-3.

Reports discovery of a bundle burial near Pierson, Montcalm County. Copper and shell beads, fabric, etc., found. Calls attention to skeletal remains and copper artifacts found in Saginaw area.

36. ——. [editor]. [no title]. The Coffinberry News-Bulletin, Vol. IV, No. 1. Wright L. Coffinberry Chapter, Michigan Archaeological Society, Grand Rapids, Jan., 1957, pp. 3-4.

Further report on above Montcalm County find.

37. Burgh, Robert. The Region of Three Oaks. Norwood, Mass. and LaPorte, Ind., Plimpton Press, 1939, 1 map.

Pages 29-34 refer to archaeological features, etc., to be found in Berrien County.

38. Burton, Clarence M., Editor-in-Chief; William Stocking, Associate Editor; and Gordon K. Miller, Associate Editor. The City of Detroit, Michigan. Detroit and Chicago, The S. J. Clarke Publishing Co., 1922, Vol. I, Chap. 2, "Prehistoric Detroit," pp. 43-44.

Includes information on Indian tribes and their remains found in the vicinity of Detroit.

39. Burton, Clarence M., and M. Agnes Burton, Editors; H. T. O. Blue and Gordon K. Miller, Associate Editors. History of Wayne County and the City of Detroit, Michigan. Detroit and Chicago, The S. J. Clarke Publishing Co., 1930, Vol. I. "Aboriginal Inhabitants," pp. 11-13.

40. Butterfield, George E., editor. Bay County. *In* Fuller, George N., Historic Michigan, Vol. III. Dayton, Ohio, National Historical Association, Inc., 1924.

Pages 17-18 briefly locate former mounds within the city limits of Bay City.

41. ——, editor. Bay County, Past and Present. Bay City, Mich., C. & J. Gregory, 1918, illus.

Locates mounds and contains one page of Bay County artifacts from a local collection. Pp. 25-28.

42. Butterfield, Ira W. Designation of Sites by the Rectangular System of the U. S. Public Lands Survey. Methods of Handling the Irregular Section of Land. Michigan Archaeological Society News, Vol. II, No. 1. Michigan Archaeological Society, Ann Arbor, Jan., 1955, pp. 7-9, 4 illus.

43. ——. Maps for Archaeological Investigations in the Great Lakes Area. Michigan Archaeologist, Vol. VI, No. 1. Michigan Archaeological Society, Grand Rapids, March, 1960, pp. 6-16.

44. Butterfield, Ira W., and Ralph W. Stroebel. Grinding on Projectile Points in Bay and Saginaw Counties, Michigan. The Totem Pole, Vol. XLIII, No. 8. Aboriginal Research Club, Detroit, Mich., Nov., 1960, 6 unnumbered pp., 3 illus.

## C

45. Caches. The Totem Pole, Vol. XI, No. 5. Aboriginal Research Club, Detroit, Mich., Aug., 1943, pp. 1-3.

A summary of entry No. 125.

46. Calkins, E. A. Old Trails of Ingham County, bound manuscript in Michigan State Library, Lansing, Mich., 1929, 6 pp.

47. Campbell, John. Recently Discovered Relics of the American Mound-Builders. Proceedings and Transactions of the Royal Society of Canada, Vol. IV, 2d Ser., Sec. II. London, England, Bernard Quaritch; Ottawa, Canada, James Hope and Son; Toronto, Canada, The Copp-Clark Company, 1898, pp. 3-19, 3 illus.

Soper "finds" discussed and inscriptions translated as in Turanian language.

48. Cannon, George H. Prehistoric Forts in Macomb County. Michigan Pioneer and Historical Collections, Vol. XXXVIII. Lansing, Mich., Wynkoop Hallenbeck Crawford Co., 1912, pp. 73-78, 4 illus., 1 map.

Describes and locates forts and mounds.

49. ——. Prehistoric Forts in Macomb County. The Totem Pole, Vol. XXII, No. 5. Aboriginal Research Club, Detroit, Mich., Feb., 1949, pp. 1-4.

A reprint from the Michigan Pioneer and Historical Collections, Vol. XXXVIII. See entry No. 48.

50. Carson, H. H. Village Trails and Mounds in Michigan. The American Antiquarian and Oriental Journal, Vol. IX, No. 4. Chicago, Ill., F. H. Revell, July, 1887, pp. 237-238.

51. Chapter Activities. Michigan Archaeological Society News, Vol. I, No. 4. Michigan Archaeological Society, Ann Arbor, Oct., 1954, pp. 1-4, 1 illus.

Surface finds, grave contents, test trench results, etc., reported by various chapters.

52. Cherry, P. P. Curious Stones from the Stone Age. District Historical Society, Tract #3. Wadsworth, Ohio, Steam Printing House, 1878, pp. 1-7, 10 illus.

Includes a letter from Wright L. Coffinberry which describes an engraved slab found at Grand Traverse Bay and a notched and perforated stone found in Gratton Township, Kent County. Both illustrated.

53. Chips from the Totem Pole. Aboriginal Research Club, Detroit, Mich., May, 1962, p. 1, 1 illus.

Illustrates a graving tool, lanceolate point and three worked fragments found at the New Paleo Site, No. 2, Sterling Township, Macomb County.

54. ——. Aboriginal Research Club, Detroit, Mich., Oct., 1962, p. 1, 1 illus.

Illustrates a Michigan barbed axe found on a farm in Delaware Township, Sanilac County.

55. ——. Aboriginal Research Club, Detroit, Mich., Nov., 1962, p. 1, 1 illus.

Brief report on further work on the DeVisscher Paleo 2 Site. See entries Nos. 53, 175, 513, 653, 654, 656, 661, 662.

56. Circular and Replies Thereto Pertaining to the Resources of Michigan. Michigan Pioneer and Historical Collections, Vol. XII. Lansing, Mich., Wynkoop Hallenbeck Crawford Co., 1908, pp. 381-406.

Results of a circular sent to various counties in order to record state resources that included prehistoric Indian mounds, garden beds, burials, etc.

57. Clancey, Mrs. James Hannibal. Some Indian Graves at Escanaba. Michigan History Magazine, Vol. VIII, No. 2. Lansing, Michigan Historical Commission, April, 1924, pp. 135-139, 3 illus.

58. Coffinberry, Wright L. Mound Explorations in Western Michigan. Original manuscript in the Grand Rapids Public Museum, Grand Rapids, Mich.

See following entry.

59. ——. The Coffinberry Manuscript—Copy. The Coffinberry News-Bulletin, Vol. IX, No. 2 through Vol. IX, No. 11. Wright L. Coffinberry Chapter, Michigan Archaeological Society, Grand Rapids, Feb.-Dec., 1962, 1 illus.

This manuscript continued and completed in subsequent 1963 issues.

60. Coffinberry, W. L., and E. A. Strong. Notes Upon Some Explorations of Ancient Mounds in the Vicinity of Grand Rapids, Mich. Proceedings of the American Association for the Advancement of Science, 24th Meeting Held at Detroit, Michigan, August 1875. Published by the Permanent Secretary, Salem, Mass., 1876, pp. 293-297.

61. C [ollins], N [ewell] E. Wapisiwisibiwininiwak. The Totem Pole, Vol. III, No. 2. Aboriginal Research Club, Detroit, Mich., May, 1939, pp. 4-5.

Site on Swan Creek, Fair Haven, described. Surface finds consisted of stone, pottery, and skeletal material. See entry No. 633.

62. ——. Replicas *vs.* Counterfeits. The Totem Pole, Vol. V, No. 2. Aboriginal Research Club, Detroit, Mich., May, 1940, p. 5.

63. ——. Another Site. The Totem Pole, Vol. IX, No. 3. Aboriginal Research Club, Detroit, Mich., June, 1942, pp. 1-2.

Indications of occupation on Swan Creek, on opposite side of site in entries Nos. 61 and 633, are described.

64. ——. Two Delta County Sites. The Totem Pole, Vol. X, No. 2. Aboriginal Research Club, Detroit, Mich., Nov., 1942, pp. 1-2.

Location, description, and surface finds of two sites on Whitefish and Sturgeon Rivers are given.

65. ——. Evidences of Use and Wear. The Totem Pole, Vol. X, No. 3. Aboriginal Research Club, Detroit, Mich., Dec., 1942, p. 1.

Waterworn artifacts found on Manitoulin Island. Discusses dating of artifacts by water levels and the significance of wear on various types of Michigan artifacts.

66. ——. A Perforated Skull. The Totem Pole, Vol. X, No. 6. Aboriginal Research Club, Detroit, Mich., March, 1943, pp. 1-5, 3 illus.

Tells of a burial and its contents found near Algonac.

67. Collins, Newell E. Perforated Indian Skulls. The Wisconsin Archeologist, Vol. XXIV, No. 3. Wisconsin Archeological Society, Milwaukee, Wis., Sept., 1943, pp. 50-53, 1 illus.

68. C [ollins], N [ewell] E. Remarkable—if True. The Totem Pole, Vol. XIV, No. 4. Aboriginal Research Club, Detroit, Mich., Jan., 1945, p. 3.

Summary of a booklet by John A. Russell on the Soper "finds." See Index.

69. ——. Personal Observations and Hearsay. The Totem Pole, Vol. XVI, No. 2. Aboriginal Research Club, Detroit, Mich., Nov., 1945, pp. 4-5.

Lists and briefly describes some sites and their contents around Lake St. Clair.

70. ——. Perforated Indian Skulls. The Totem Pole, Vol. XXVII, No. 4. Aboriginal Research Club, Detroit, Mich., July, 1951, pp. 1-4.

Reviews perforated skulls found in Michigan and Canada up to 1951.

71. Collins, Newell E. Indians with Holes in Their Heads. The Totem Pole, Vol. XXXVII, No. 3. Aboriginal Research Club, Algonac, Mich., Dec., 1955, pp. 1-6.

72. A Copper Pickax Found. The American Antiquarian and Oriental Journal, Vol. XXIV, No. 5. Chicago, Ill., Stephen D. Peet, Sept.-Oct., 1902, p. 421.

Describes a copper axe found on the shore of Lake Gogebic, which is in Ontonagon and Gogebic Counties.

73. Cornelius, Eldon S. Lee Site No. 1. The Totem Pole, Vol. XL, No. 5. Aboriginal Research Club, Detroit, Mich., Dec., 1957, 8 unnumbered pp., 4 illus.

74. ——. The Porter Site 11. The Totem Pole, Vol. XLI, No. 7. Aboriginal Research Club, Detroit, Mich., Oct., 1958, 2 unnumbered pp., 2 illus.

75. ——. Leo Linseman [sic] Mound Group. The Totem Pole, Vol. XLI, No. 8. Aboriginal Research Club, Detroit, Mich., Nov., 1958, 4 unnumbered pp., 2 illus.

76. ——. Jerome Site #2. The Totem Pole, Vol. XLI, No. 8. Aboriginal Research Club, Detroit, Mich., Nov., 1958, 1 unnumbered page, 1 illus.

77. ——. Midland Site No. 12. The Totem Pole, Vol. XLIII, No. 7. Aboriginal Research Club, Detroit, Mich., Oct., 1959, 4 unnumbered pp., 2 illus.

78. ——. Surface Indications of Lodge Sites. The Totem Pole, Vol. XLIII, No. 5. Aboriginal Research Club, Detroit, Mich., May, 1960, 6 unnumbered pp., 4 illus.

79. ——. Stone Configuration in Gladwin County. The Totem Pole, Vol. XLIV, No. 2. Aboriginal Research Club, Detroit, Mich., Feb., 1961, 3 unnumbered pp., 2 illus.

80. Cornelius, Eldon S., and Harold W. Moll. Locating the Post Molds of Lodges on Sites from Surface Indications. Michigan Archaeologist, Vol. V, No. 1. Michigan Archaeological Society, Ann Arbor, March, 1959, pp. 1-2.

81. ——. The Walters-Linsenman Earthwork Site. The Totem Pole, Vol. XLIV, No. 9. Aboriginal Research Club, Detroit, Mich., Dec., 1961, pp. 1-9, 2 illus.

82. Cornell, M. E. Prehistoric Relics of the Mound Builders. [Publisher?] Battle Creek, Mich., (n.d.), pp. 32, 3 illus.

An account of the Soper "finds." See Index.

83. Crane, H. R. University of Michigan Radiocarbon Dates I. Science, Vol. CXXIV, No. 3224. American Association for the Advancement of Science, Lancaster, Pa., Oct., 1956, pp. 664-672.

84. Crane, H. R., and James B. Griffin. University of Michigan Radiocarbon Dates II. Science, Vol. CXXVII, No. 3306. American Association for the Advancement of Science, Lancaster, Pa., May, 1958, pp. 1098-1105.

85. ——. University of Michigan Radiocarbon Dates III. Science, Vol. CXXVIII, No. 3332. American Association for the Advancement of Science, Lancaster, Pa., Nov., 1958, pp. 1117-1123.

86. ——. University of Michigan Radiocarbon Dates IV. American Journal of Science Radiocarbon Supplement, Vol. I. New Haven, Conn., Yale University Press, 1959, pp. 173-198.

87. Cunningham, Wilbur M., with an appendix by James B. Griffin. A Study of the Glacial Kame Culture in Michigan, Ohio and Indiana. Occasional Contributions from the Museum of Anthropology of the University of Michigan, No. 12. Ann Arbor, University of Michigan, 1948, 11 illus., 1 map.

88. ——. Glacial Kame Artifacts from Michigan and Ohio. Ohio Archaeologist, Vol. VIII, No. 4. The Archaeological Society of Ohio, Dayton, Oct., 1958, pp. 133-136, 2 illus.

89. Cunningham, W[ilbur] M. Shell Gorget Type Perforations in Slate. Ohio Archaeologist, Vol. VII, No. 3-4. The Archaeological Society of Ohio, Columbus, July-Oct., 1962, pp. 104-105, 1 illus.

Raises questions of origin, form, and function of slate gorgets. Five are illustrated, three of which are from Michigan.

90. Cushman, Gwynne. The Bristol Site. The Totem Pole, Vol. XLII, No. 6. Aboriginal Research Club, Detroit, Mich., June, 1959, 6 unnumbered pp., 5 illus.

91. ——. Another Mason County Site. The Totem Pole, Vol. XLV, No. 7. Aboriginal Research Club, Detroit, Mich., Oct., 1962, 4 unnumbered pp., 3 illus.

## D

92. Davis, A. C. Antiquities of Isle Royale, Lake Superior. Annual Report, Smithsonian Institution, 1874. Washington, D. C., Government Printing Office, 1875, pp. 369-370.

> Description given of a mass of copper found in an ancient mine pit with large number of hammerstones and quantities of ashes and charcoal.

93. ——. Antiquities of Isle Royale, Lake Superior. *In* Drier, Roy Ward, and Octave Joseph Du Temple, editors. Prehistoric Copper Mining in the Lake Superior Region: A Collection of Reference Articles. Calumet, Mich., Drier and DuTemple, 1961, p. 85. See entry No. 110.

94. Davis, George W., and Edward V. Gillis. Archaeological Excavations of the Parson Mound Group, Brooks Township [,] Newaygo County, Michigan. Unpublished manuscript in the Grand Rapids Public Library, Grand Rapids, Mich., Oct., 1954, 29 typewritten pp., 89 illus., 1 map.

95. ——. Grand Traverse Bay Archaic. The Coffinberry News Bulletin, Vol. VI, No. 6. Wright L. Coffinberry Chapter, Michigan Archaeological Society, Grand Rapids, June, 1959, pp. 66-70, 3 illus.

96. De Casson, Dollier, and De Bréhant de Galinée, edited and translated by James H. Coyne. Exploration of the Great Lakes, 1669-1670. Galinée's Narrative and Map. Ontario Historical Society, Vol. IV, Pt. 1. Published by the Society, Toronto, Canada, 1903, p. 67, 1 map.

> Gives the description and location of a stone idol on the Detroit River that was venerated by the Indians and destroyed by this exploring party.

97. De Galinee, Rene de Brehant. Old Mariner's Shrine on Detroit River. Michigan Archaeologist, Vol. IV, No. 4. Michigan Archaeological Society, Ann Arbor, Dec., 1958, pp. 70-73.

> Excerpt from De Galinee's narrative of an expedition from Montreal to Sault Ste Marie (1669-1670) referring to a sacrificial rock formerly on the shore of the Detroit River. Also locates shell heaps on the bank of the Flint River, in or near Richfield, Genesee County. Specimens of shells deposited with U. S. National Museum.

98. De Nadaillac, Marquis, translated by N. D'Anvers, W. H. Hall, editor. Prehistoric America. New York, G. P. Putnam's Sons, 1884.

Mentions mounds, p. 82; pottery, p. 138; collar of bear teeth, copper and bird bone beads, p. 172; circular mound on Detroit River, p. 175; description of copper mining on Lake Superior, pp. 178-180.

99. ——, translated by Nancy Bell (N. D'Anvers). Manners and Monuments of Prehistoric Peoples. New York, G. P. Putnam's Sons, 1892.

Mention of a jade hatchet from Michigan, p. 284.

100. De Visscher, Jerry. Three Macomb County "Copper and Mica" Burials. The Totem Pole, Vol. XL, No. 4. Aboriginal Research Club, Detroit, Mich., Oct., 1957, 5 unnumbered pp., 3 illus.

101. Dockstader, Frederick J. [compiler]. The American Indian in Graduate Studies [;] A Bibliography of Theses and Dissertations. Contributions from the Museum of the American Indian, Heye Foundation, Vol. XV. Museum of American Indian, Heye Foundation, New York, N. Y., 1957, pp. 399.

102. Dodge, Byron E. The Antiquarian, Vol. I, Pt. 7. Columbus, Ohio, The Landon Printing and Publishing Co., July, 1897, pp. 191-192.

Gives measurements and contents of a mound opened in 1896 in Oregon Township, Lapeer County. Finds include 14 skeletons.

103. ——. The American Archaeologist, Vol. II, Pt. 3. Columbus, Ohio, The Landon Printing and Publishing Co., March, 1898, p. 78.

Records the presence of a row of stepping stones to form a bridge in the bed of the Flint River, Genesee Township, Genesee County. [Of Indian origin?]

104. ——. The American Archaeologist, Vol. II, Pt. 11. Columbus, Ohio. The Landon Printing and Publishing Co., Nov., 1898, p. 299.

Tells of shell heaps on bank of Flint River in or near Richfield, Genesee County. Some shells deposited in U. S. National Museum.

105. Doty, Tom. Some Ionia County Relics. The Totem Pole, Vol. XLV, No. 8. Aboriginal Research Club, Detroit, Mich., Nov., 1962, 2 unnumbered pp., 2 illus.

106. Drier, Roy Ward. Michigan's Most Ancient Industry. Inside Michigan, Vol. III, No. 7. Ann Arbor and Detroit, Inside Michigan Publishers, Inc., July, 1953, pp. 15-17, 3 illus., 1 map.

107. ——. Michigan's Most Ancient Industry. *In* Drier, Roy Ward, and Octave Joseph Du Temple, editors. Prehistoric Copper Mining in the Lake Superior Region: A Collection of Reference Articles. Calumet, Mich., Drier and Du Temple, 1961, pp. 1925.

See entry No. 110.

108. ——. Archaeology and Some Metallurgical Investigative Techniques. *In* Griffin, James B., editor. Lake Superior Copper and the Indians, Anthropological Papers, No. 17, Museum of Anthropology, University of Michigan, Ann Arbor, University of Michigan, 1961, pp. 134-147.

See entry No. 289.

109. ——— . The Michigan College of Mining and Technology Isle Royale Excavations, 1953-1954. *In* Griffin, James B., Editor. Lake Superior Copper and the Indians, Anthropological papers, No. 17, Museum of Anthropology, University of Michigan, 1961, pp. 1-76.

See Entry No. 289.

110. Drier, Roy Ward, and Octave Joseph Du Temple, editors. Prehistoric Copper Mining in the Lake Superior Region: A Collection of Reference Articles. Calumet, Mich., Drier and Du Temple, 1961, pp. 213, 20 illus., 11 maps.

111. Duchaine, William J., H. W. Kuhm, C. E. Brown. Isle Royale National Park. The Wisconsin Archeologist, Vol. XV, No. 1. Wisconsin Archeological Society, Milwaukee, July, 1935, pp. 12-18.

Presentation of the flora, fauna, geology, and copper mines of Isle Royale.

112. Durant, Samuel W. History of Ingham and Eaton Counties, Michigan. Philadelphia, D. W. Ensign and Co., 1880, Chap. 2, "Prehistoric," pp. 21-23.

113. ——— . History of Kalamazoo County. Philadelphia, Everts and Abbott, 1880.

On pages 65-68 is an illustrated discussion of garden beds as well as other archaeological data.

114. Dustin, Fred. Saginaw County as a Center of Aboriginal Population. Michigan Historical Collections, Vol. XXXIX. Michigan Historical Commission, Lansing, Mich., 1915, pp. 251-260.

115. ——— . Materials of the Indian Lapidary in the Saginaw District, Michigan. Papers of the Michigan Academy of Science, Arts, and Letters, Vol. VIII. New York, The Macmillan Co., 1928, pp. 11-22.

116. ——— . Some Ancient Fire-Beds in Saginaw County, Michigan. Michigan History Magazine, Vol. XIII, No. 2. Michigan Historical Commission, Lansing, Mich., 1929, pp. 301-307.

117. ——— . Ancient Pottery Remains in the Saginaw District, Michigan. Papers of the Michigan Academy of Science, Arts, and Letters, Vol. X. Ann Arbor, University of Michigan Press, 1929, pp. 69-77.

118. ——— . Some Ancient Indian Village Sites in Saginaw County, Michigan. Papers of the Michigan Academy of Science, Arts, and Letters, Vol. XII. Ann Arbor, University of Michigan Press, 1930, pp. 75-93, 1 map.

119. ——— . Indian Pipes Collected in Saginaw County, Michigan. Papers of the Michigan Academy of Science, Arts, and Letters, Vol. XIV. Ann Arbor, University of Michigan Press, 1931, pp. 35-45, 2 illus.

120. ——— . Report on Indian Earthworks in Ogemaw County, Michigan. Scientific Publication, No. 1, Cranbrook Institute of Science, Bloomfield Hills, Mich., 1932, pp. 1-25.

121. ——— . A Summary of the Archaeology of Isle Royale, Michigan. Papers of the Michigan Academy of Science, Arts, and Letters, Vol. XVI. Ann Arbor, University of Michigan Press, 1932, pp. 1-16, 3 illus., 1 map.

122. ——— . A Study of the Bayport Chert. Papers of the Michigan Academy of Science, Arts, and Letters, Vol. XX. Ann Arbor, University of Michigan Press, 1935, pp. 465-475.

123. ——— . Some Pioneers of Michigan Archaeology. Michigan History Magazine, Vol. XX. Spring and Summer No. Michigan Historical Commission, Lansing, 1936, pp. 213-219.

A brief review of the history of Michigan archaeology up to the time of Wilbert B. Hinsdale. Also gives the details of the founding of the Michigan Archaeological Society.

124. ——— . Prehistoric Storage Pits in Saginaw County, Michigan. Papers of the Michigan Academy of Science, Arts, and Letters, Vol. XXI. Ann Arbor, University of Michigan Press, 1936, pp. 7-11, 3 illus., 2 maps.

125. ——— . Caches of Prehistoric Artifacts Discovered in Saginaw County, Michigan. Papers of the Michigan Academy of Science, Arts, and Letters, Vol. XXVII. Ann Arbor, University of Michigan Press, 1942, pp. 505-510.

126. ——— . Saginaw History, Part I, The Prehistoric Period, prepared for the Board of Directors of the Saginaw Museum, 1949. Bound, typed manuscript at Michigan State Library, Lansing, 202 pp.

127. ——— . An Archaeological Reconnaissance of Isle Royale. Michigan History, Vol. XLI, No. 1. Michigan Historical Commission, Lansing, March, 1957, pp. 1-34, 4 illus., 1 map.

E

128. Early Man. American Antiquity, Vol. XIX, No. 1. The Society for American Archaeology, Salt Lake City, Utah, July, 1953, pp. 100-101.

Refers to Imlay City eoliths found by Carmen Baggerly. See entry No. 8.

129. Eldredge, Robert F. Past and Present of Macomb County, Michigan. Chicago, S. J. Clarke Publishing Co., 1905. Chap. 1, "Historical," pp. 543-547.

Includes the location and description of mounds and forts.

130. The Eliza Howell Park Site. The Totem Pole, Vol. VI, No. 3. Aboriginal Research Club, Detroit, Mich., Dec., 1940, 3 unnumbered pp.

Gives the location of the site and tells of the artifacts excavated at the Eliza Howell Park, on River Rouge, Detroit.

131. Ellis, Franklin. History of Genesee County, Michigan. Philadelphia, Everts and Abbott, 1879, Chap. 2, "The White Man's Predecessors in the Saginaw Valley," pp. 11-13.

132. ——— . History of Shiawassee and Clinton Counties, Michigan. Philadelphia, D. W. Ensign and Co., 1880, Chap. 1, "Indian History of the Two Counties," pp. 9-17.

133. Ellis, Holmes H. Surface Exposures of Flint and Chert in Michigan. Michigan Archaeologist, Vol. VI, No. 4. Michigan Archaeological Society, Ann Arbor, Dec., 1960, pp. 56-67.

134. Etzenhouser, Rudolf. Engravings of Prehistoric Specimens from Michigan, U. S. A. Detroit, John Bornman & Son, 1910, pp. 39, 44 illus.

Details of Soper "finds." See Index.

135. Exploration. Sixth Annual Report—Peabody Museum of American Archaeology and Ethnology, Vol. I. Harvard College, Cambridge, Mass., 1873, pp. 12-13.

Briefly describes and tells of the purchase from Henry Gillman of the contents of a mound on the Detroit River.

136. Explorations. Reports of the Peabody Museum of American Archaeology and Ethnology, Harvard University, Vol. I, 1868-1876. Printed by order of the Board of Trustees, Cambridge, Mass., 1876, pp. 12-13.

Reports purchase of a collection of artifacts (shells, copper, antler, pottery, etc.) and human remains from a mound on the Detroit River.

## F

137. Fair Haven Burial. The Totem Pole, Vol. XIII, No. 4. Aboriginal Research Club, Detroit, Mich., July, 1944, p. 5.

Brief description given of a burial and its contents at the Fair Haven Meyers Site, Fair Haven, Mich.

138. Ferguson, William P. F. Michigan's Most Ancient Industry: The Prehistoric Mines and Miners of Isle Royale. Michigan History Magazine, Vol. VII, No. 3-4. Michigan Historical Commission, Lansing, July-Oct., 1923, pp. 155-162, 2 illus.

139. ———. The Franklin Isle Royale Expedition. Michigan History Magazine, Vol. VIII, No. 4. Michigan Historical Commission, Lansing, 1924, pp. 450-468, 3 illus., 1 map.

Report of an expedition to study the ancient copper mines on Isle Royale.

140. ———. Michipicoten. 35th Annual Archaeological Report, 1924-1925, Being Part of Appendix to the Report of the Minister of Education, Ontario. Printed by order of the Legislative Assembly of Ontario, Toronto, Canada, 1927, pp. 31-33.

Outlines the archaeological similarity of Michipicoten and Isle Royale.

141. Find of Indian Skeletons. The American Antiquarian and Oriental Journal, Vol. XVI, No. 6. Good Hope, Ill., Stephen D. Peet, Dec., 1894, p. 383.

A Grosse Isle burial reported from which two skeletons, two pipes, a tomahawk, and trade silver were recovered.

142. Fire-Cracked Stones. Michigan Archaeological Society News, Vol. II, No. 3. Michigan Archaeological Society, Ann Arbor, Aug., 1956, pp. 2-3.

143. Fisher, A. W. Cache of Leaf-Shaped Relics. Popular Science, Vol. XXXV, No. 2. New York, Lillard & Co., Feb., 1901, p. 38.

144. Fisher, Ernest B., editor. Grand Rapids and Kent County, Michigan. Chicago, Robert O. Law Co., 1918, Vol. I, Chap. 1, "Prehistoric," pp. 17-21.

145. Foote, Edward A. Historical Sketch of the Early Days of Eaton County. Michigan Pioneer and Historical Collections, Vol. III. Lansing, Robert Smith Printing Co., 1903, pp. 379-431.

Tells of Indian corn fields on site of present cities of Charlotte, Walton, and Eaton as well as the location of village sites and burial grounds.

146. Fort Wayne Mound, Detroit. Michigan Archaeologist, Vol. VI, No. 1. Michigan Archaeological Society, Grand Rapids, March, 1960, p. 17.

147. Foster, J. W. On the Antiquity of Man in North America. Transactions of the Chicago Academy of Sciences, Vol. I, Pt. 1. Published by the Academy, Chicago, Ill., 1867-1869, pp. 227-257.

Describes prehistoric copper mining of the mound builders in Michigan.

148. —— , and J. D. Whitney. Report on the Geology and Topography of a Portion of the Lake Superior Land District in the State of Michigan. Executive Document No. 69, Pt. 1. Printed for the House of Representatives, Washington, D. C., 1850, pp. 158-163, 3 illus.

Presents the evidence and extent of ancient mining in the Ontonagon region, at Keweenaw Point and on Isle Royale.

149. Fox, George R. An Archeological Survey of Cass County, Michigan. Unpublished manuscript in the Grand Rapids Public Library, Grand Rapids, Mich. (n.d.) 20 unnumbered pp., 9 illus., 7 maps.

Covers Cass County trails, village sites, mounds, burials, garden beds, artifacts, etc.

150. —— . The Archeology of Michigan. *In* Fuller, George N., Historic Michigan, Vol III. Dayton, O., National Historical Association, Inc., 1924. "Land of the Great Lakes," pp. 22-42.

151. —— . The Ancient Copper Workings on Isle Royale. The Wisconsin Archeologist, [O.S.], Vol. X, No. 2. Wisconsin Archeological Society, Milwaukee, July-Oct., 1911, pp. 73-100, 14 illus.

152. —— . A Minor Mystery of Michigan Archeology. Michigan History Magazine, Vol. IV, No. 2-3 (Whole #13). Michigan Historical Commission, Lansing, 1920, pp. 583-587, 4 illus.

Details are given of a stone, sand, clay and charcoal-lined pit the use of which is problematical.

153. ——— . What About Michigan Archeology? Michigan History Magazine, Vol. VI, No. 2-3. Michigan Historical Commission, Lansing, 1922, pp. 415-434, 3 maps.

Reviews status of Michigan archaeology, as well as work and publishing done. Includes three maps of the Lower Peninsula that show mounds, earthworks, enclosures, circles, and garden beds.

154. ——— . The Archeology of Michigan. Michigan History Magazine, Vol. VIII, No. 3. Michigan Historical Commission, Lansing, July, 1924, pp. 314-348, 4 maps.

155. ——— . Isle Royale Expedition. Michigan History Magazine, Vol. XIII, No. 2. Michigan Historical Commission, Lansing, 1929, pp. 308-323, 6 illus.

An account of the McDonald-Massee Isle Royale expedition to study prehistoric copper mining.

156. ——— . The Ancient Copper Workings on Isle Royale (Conclusions Only). *In* The Ancient Copper Mines of Northern Michigan, The Wisconsin Archeologist, Vol. X, No. 2, July-Oct., 1911, Aboriginal Research Club, Detroit, Mich. (1941)?, p. 96.

157. ——— . The Prehistoric Garden Beds of Wisconsin and Michigan and the Fox Indians. The Wisconsin Archeologist, Vol. XL, No. 1. Wisconsin Archeological Society, Milwaukee, March, 1959, pp. 1-19, 2 maps.

158. ——— . Michigan's Largest Arrow. The Totem Pole, Vol. XLIII, No. 7. Aboriginal Research Club, Detroit, Mich., Oct., 1960, 5 unnumbered pp., 1 illus.

159. ——— . A History of the Founding of the First Archeological Society in Michigan. The Coffinberry News Bulletin, Vol. VII, No. 11. Wright L. Coffinberry Chapter, Michigan Archaeological Society, Grand Rapids, Dec., 1960, pp. 124-126.

160. Franz, Harvey, editor. News Letter, Vol. II, No. 1. Southwest Chapter, Michigan Archaeological Society, Benton Harbor, June, 1954, p. 1,

Reports the finding of a flint fishhook near South Haven and the discovery of a mortar near Lacota.

161. ——— , editor. News Letter, Vol. II, No. 3. Southwest Chapter, Michigan Archaeological Society, Benton Harbor, June, 1954, pp. 1-2.

Tells of the digging into and measuring of, the "horseshoe" on a farm at Summerville, Cass County. Disturbed soil, flint chips, and artifacts were found.

162. ——— , editor. Separate page inserted between Nos. 3 and 4, Vol. III. News Letter, Southwest Chapter, Michigan Archaeological Society, Benton Harbor, Aug. or Sept., 1955, p. 1.

Fifty-nine storage pits located and mapped on a farm in Penn Township, Cass County.

163. —— , editor. News Letter, Vol. III, No. 4. Southwest Chapter, Michigan Archaeological Society, Benton Harbor, Sept., 1955, pp. 1-2.

> Reports the finding of a bone awl, pottery pipe stem, broken bone, and charcoal when pits in entry No. 161 were excavated.

164. —— , editor. News Letter, Vol. IV, No. 7. Southwest Chapter, Michigan Archaeological Society, Benton Harbor, Oct., 1956, p. 1.

> Brief description of the excavations on the Barron Lake Mound. Human bone (skull fragments and teeth), pieces of shell and an arrowpoint were found. Also reports results of the opening of some mounds in the same area in Cass County in 1834.

165. —— , editor. News Letter, Vol. IV, No. 8. Southwest Chapter, Michigan Archaeological Society, Benton Harbor, Nov., 1956, p. 2.

> Report by George Fox on a Cass County mound opened before 1900 and containing seven or more skeletons buried in cartwheel style. Refers to two other mounds in the same county opened in latter part of the last century with similar burials.

166. —— , editor. News Letter, Vol. VI, No. 3. Southwest Chapter, Michigan Archaeological Society, Benton Harbor, Aug., 1958, pp. 1-2.

> "Placer mining" for artifacts in soil removed for a basement north of Berrien Springs. Finds include human bone fragments, copper gorget, and 300 arrowpoints. Also reports finding of silver ornaments, six lockets, 30 brooches, beads, 12 crosses, etc., on west bank of St. Joseph River opposite the site of Fort St. Joseph.

167. —— , editor. News Letter, Vol. VI, No. 4. Southwest Chapter, Michigan Archaeological Society, Benton Harbor, Sept., 1958, p. 1.

> One hundred and eleven more arrowpoints found at Berrien Springs construction excavation above. Also reports surface finds found south of Baroda some years earlier.

168. —— , editor. News Letter, Vol. VII, No. 4. Southwest Chapter, Michigan Archaeological Society, Benton Harbor, Aug., 1959, p. 1.

> Notes finding of arrowpoints, scrapers, and pot shreds at a camp site on north bank of School Section Lake, Hartford.

169. —— , editor. News Letter, Vol. VIII, No. 3. Southwest Chapter, Michigan Archaeological Society, Benton Harbor, July, 1960, p. 1.

> Reports discovery of triangular arrow points at Garlanger-Ross site.

170. —— , editor. News Letter, Vol. VIII, No. 9. Southwest Chapter, Michigan Archaeological Society, Benton Harbor, April, 1961, p. 2.

> Quotes Wright L. Coffinberry Chapter "News Letter," Michigan Archaeological Society, (n.d.), on the bringing out of a 175 - pound double-grooved hammerstone from Owl Creek Canyon [location?].

171. —— , editor. News Letter, Vol. IX, No. 2. Southwest Chapter, Michigan Archaeological Society, Benton Harbor, July, 1961, p. 1.

Describes and locates a disturbed double burial found on a farm in the vicinity of Benton Harbor.

172. —— , editor. News Letter, Vol. X, No. 3. Southwest Chapter, Michigan Archaeological Society, Benton Harbor, July, 1962, p. 1.

Tells of the uncovering by a construction crew in Grandville of four burials and parts of two others as well as trade goods of brass, iron, and silver.

173. Frauds in Michigan. The American Antiquarian and Oriental Journal, Vol. XVI, No. 6. Good Hope, Ill., Stephen D. Peet, Dec., 1894, p. 384.

A letter stating that frauds being found are in same locality that "Assyrian and Egyptian faces" had been discovered a few years previously. See Soper "finds" in Index.

174. Fredeen, H. E. The Story of Isle Royale. Michigan History Magazine, Vol. XXV, Autumn No. Michigan Historical Commission, Lansing, 1941, pp. 330-353.

Brief review of archaeological finds by local individuals on the island. Tells of the discoveries of the Milwaukee Public Museum Expedition of 1928.

175. Further Test Digging at the New Paleo Site (No. 2). Chips from the Totem Pole, Aboriginal Research Club, Detroit, Mich., Jan., 1962, p. 1, 1 illus.

Illustrates twelve artifacts found at the site in Sterling Township, Macomb County. See entries Nos. 53, 55, 513, 653, 654, 656, 661, 662.

## G

176. Gansser, Augustus H., editor. History of Bay County, Michigan and Representative Citizens. Chicago, Richmond and Arnold, 1905, Chap. IV, Early Settlements and Settlers, pp. 60-98.

Locations, dimensions and contents of Bay County mounds given, as well as a description of some local artifacts and the burial of an Indian in a mound in the early 19th century.

177. Gibbs, Morris. Origin of Mounds. Popular Science, Vol. XXXIII, No. 3. New York, Lillard & Co., March, 1899, p. 59.

Gives a detailed account of the mound formerly on an island in the Kalamazoo River, near Comstock.

178. Gibson, Edmond P. Ancient Mounds Near Grand Rapids in the Lower Grand River Valley and in Southwestern Michigan. Michigan Archaeological Society News, Vol. I, No. 3. Michigan Archaeological Society, Ann Arbor, June, 1954, pp. 3-10.

Extract given from Wright L. Coffinberry's report in entry No. 60. Also describes the opening of two mounds of the Norton group in 1915. Other mounds and their contents in the vicinity of Grand Rapids described in detail.

179. ——— . [no title]. Ohio Archaeologist, Vol. VII, No. 4. The Archaeological Society of Ohio, Dayton, Oct., 1957, pp. 147-148.

A good summary of the Soper "finds." See Index.

180. ——— . Indian Sites Along Grand River in Ottawa County Part I. The Coffinberry News Bulletin, Vol. V, No. 11. Wright L. Coffinberry Chapter, Michigan Archaeological Society, Grand Rapids, Dec., 1958, pp. 4-6, 1 map.

181. ——— . Indian Sites Along Grand River in Ottawa County Part II. The Coffinberry News Bulletin, Vol. VI, No. 1. Wright L. Coffinberry Chapter, Michigan Archaeological Society, Grand Rapids, Jan., 1959, pp. 2-4, 1 map.

182. ——— . The Norton Mounds in Wyoming Township, Kent County, Michigan. Michigan Archaeologist, Vol. V, No. 2. Michigan Archaeological Society, Ann Arbor, June, 1959, pp. 20-38, 6 illus.

183. ——— . The Prehistoric Earthworks at Hamilton, Mich. The Coffinberry News Bulletin, Vol. VI, No. 7. Wright L. Coffinberry Chapter, Michigan Archaeological Society, Grand Rapids, July-Aug., 1959, pp. 72-74, 1 map.

184. ——— . The Tamarack Creek Burial. The Coffinberry News Bulletin, Vol. VII, No. 9. Wright L. Coffinberry Chapter, Michigan Archaeological Society, Grand Rapids, Oct., 1960, pp. 103-104.

185. Gibson, E[dmond] P., and Ruth Herrick. Spot Hunting in Missaukee County, Michigan. Michigan Archaeologist, Vol. III, No. 4. Michigan Archaeological Society, Ann Arbor, Dec., 1957, pp. 94-96.

186. Gibson, Edmond P., Donald Peru,and Ruth Herrick. The de Marsac Trading Post. Michigan Archaeologist, Vol. VI, No. 3. Michigan Archaeological Society, Grand Rapids, Sept., 1960, pp. 42-53, 2 illus.

187. Gifts. Reports of the Peabody Museum of American Archaeology and Ethnology, Harvard University, Vol. I, 1868-1876. Printed by order of the Board of Trustees, Cambridge, Mass., 1876, p. 11.

Records the receipt of a collection of crania and other human bones, stone implements, pottery, etc., from Michigan mounds.

188. [Gillis, Edward V.], editor. The Freye Copper Site. The Coffinberry News Bulletin, Vol. V, No. 4. Wright L. Coffinberry Chapter, Michigan Archaeological Society, Grand Rapids, April, 1958, pp. 1-4, 4 illus.

189. ——— . Ancient Skull. The Coffinberry News Bulletin, Vol. V, No. 6. Wright L. Coffinberry Chapter, Michigan Archaeological Society, Grand Rapids, June, 1958, p. 6.

Human skull, identified as almost 10,000 years old, found in Waterford Township, Oakland County, peat bog.

190. ——— . Indian Trade Silver. The Coffinberry News Bulletin, Vol. V, No. 7. Wright L. Coffinberry Chapter, Michigan Archaeological Society, Grand Rapids, July, 1958, p. 8, 1 illus.

191. Gillis, Edward V., editor. The Coffinberry News Bulletin, Vol. V, No. 8. Wright L. Coffinberry Chapter, Michigan Archaeological Society, Grand Rapids, Aug.-Sept., 1958, p. 10, 1 illus.

Illustrates with text four types of birdstones found in Michigan.

192. ——— . Quadrilobate Vessels from Western Michigan Hopewellian Culture. The Coffinberry News Bulletin, Vol. V., No. 10. Wright L. Coffinberry Chapter, Michigan Archaeological Society, Grand Rapids, Nov., 1958, p. 12, 1 illus.

Two western Michigan Hopewellian quadrilobate pottery vessels illustrated and described.

193. ——— . Types of Axes Found in Mich. The Coffinberry News Bulletin, Vol. VI, No. 2. Wright L. Coffinberry Chapter, Michigan Archaeological Society, Grand Rapids, Feb., 1959, p. 22, 1 illus.

194. ——— . Paleo-Indian Type Points. The Coffinberry News Bulletin, Vol. VI, No. 3. Wright L. Coffinberry Chapter, Michigan Archaeological Society, Grand Rapids, March, 1959, p. 34, 1 illus.

195. ——— . Editorial—Michigan Archeology Stunted? The Coffinberry News Bulletin, Vol. VI, No. 4. Wright L. Coffinberry Chapter, Michigan Archaeological Society, Grand Rapids, April, 1959, p. 45.

Discusses legal problems involved in the recovery of archaeological material on state lands.

196. ——— . The Coffinberry News Bulletin, Vol. VI, No. 4. Wright L. Coffinberry Chapter, Michigan Archaeological Society, Grand Rapids, April, 1959, p. 46, 1 illus.

Illustrates four types of slate gorgets found in Michigan.

197. ——— . The Converse Site. The Coffinberry News Bulletin, Vol. VI, No. 5. Wright L. Coffinberry Chapter, Michigan Archaeological Society, Grand Rapids, May, 1959, pp. 53-54.

198. ——— . Stone Axe. The Coffinberry News Bulletin, Vol. VI, No. 5. Wright L. Coffinberry Chapter, Michigan Archaeological Society, Grand Rapids, May, 1959, p. 58, 1 illus.

199. ——— . Archeology Can Be Dangerous. The Coffinberry News Bulletin, Vol. VI, No. 7. Wright L. Coffinberry Chapter, Michigan Archaeological Society, Grand Rapids, July-Aug., 1959, pp. 79-80.

200. ——— . Nomenclature of an Arrow Point. The Coffinberry News Bulletin, Vol. VI, No. 7. Wright L. Coffinberry Chapter, Michigan Archaeological Society, Grand Rapids, July-Aug., 1959, p. 82, 1 illus.

201. ——— . Excavation at Fort Michilimackinac, Mackinaw City. The Coffinberry News Bulletin, Vol. VI, No. 8. Wright L. Coffinberry Chapter, Michigan Archaeological Society, Grand Rapids, Sept., 1959, pp. 86-90.

202. Gillis, E[dward] V. Lure of the Copper County. The Coffinberry News Bulletin, Vol. VI, No. 8. Wright L. Coffinberry Chapter, Michigan Archaeological Society, Grand Rapids, Sept., 1959, pp. 93-95.

An introduction to the article on the same subject below. See entry No. 206.

203. [Gillis, Edward V.], editor. Haieght Mound Excavation. The Coffinberry News Bulletin, Vol. VI, No. 10. Wright L. Coffinberry Chapter, Michigan Archaeological Society, Grand Rapids, Nov., 1959, p. 119.

204. ——— . The Coffinberry News Bulletin, Vol. VI, No. 10. Wright L. Coffinberry Chapter, Michigan Archaeological Society, Grand Rapids, Nov., 1959, p. 120, 1 illus.

Illustrates, with text, two Hopewellian pottery vessels from Spoonville Mounds, Ottawa County, and Converse Mounds, Grand Rapids.

205. ——— . Bone Awls and Pottery Types. The Coffinberry News Bulletin, Vol. VI, No. 11. Wright L. Coffinberry Chapter, Michigan Archaeological Society, Grand Rapids, Dec., 1959, p. 130, 1 illus.

Illustrates four bone awls and six pottery rim sherd types found at Spring Creek Site, Muskegon County.

206. Gillis, E[dward] V. The Copper Country. The Coffinberry News Bulletin, Vol. VII, No. 1. Wright L. Coffinberry Chapter, Michigan Archaeological Society, Grand Rapids, Jan., 1960, pp. 3-17, 20, 6 illus., 1 map.

Detailed account of the archaeology of the copper country. See entry No. 202.

207. [Gillis, Edward V.], editor. The Coffinberry News Bulletin, Vol. VII, No. 2. Wright L. Coffinberry Chapter, Michigan Archaeological Society, Grand Rapids, Feb., 1960, p. 34, 1 illus.

Surface finds from Recreation Point Site, Central Lake, Antrim County, consisting of eight chipped artifacts and a copper knife, illustrated in full size.

208. Gillis, E[dward] V., editor. The Daniel De Marsac Exhibit. The Coffinberry News Bulletin, Vol. VII, No. 3. Wright L. Coffinberry Chapter, Michigan Archaeological Society, Grand Rapids, March, 1960, pp. 45-46.

Describes some of the things found at the De Marsac trading post on the Grand River at Lowell.

209. ——— . Dune Country Archeology. The Coffinberry News Bulletin, Vol. VII, No. 4. Wright L. Coffinberry Chapter, Michigan Archaeological Society, Grand Rapids, April, 1960, pp. 54-56, 1 illus.

Article includes an illustration of artifacts from the Silver Lake Site No. II, including pottery, chipped stone, bone and a clay pipe.

210. [Gillis, Edward V.], editor. The Coffinberry News Bulletin, Vol. VII, No. 6. Wright L. Coffinberry Chapter, Michigan Archaeological Society, Grand Rapids, June 1960, p. 76, 1 illus.

Illustrates, in full size, pottery and projectile point types found at Grass River Site, Antrim County.

211. Gillis, E[dward] V. Progress Report on Archeological Field Activities in Michigan by The University of Michigan, Summer of 1960. The Coffinberry News Bulletin, Vol. VII, No. 7. Wright L. Coffinberry Chapter, Michigan Archaeological Society, Grand Rapids, July-Aug., 1960, pp. 83-87.

212. [Gillis, Edward V.], editor. Crockery Creek Artifacts. The Coffinberry News Bulletin, Vol. VII, No. 7. Wright L. Coffinberry Chapter, Michigan Archaeological Society, Grand Rapids, July-Aug., 1960, p. 88, 1 illus.

213. —— . Progress Report on Archeological Excavations at Fort Michilimackinac, Mackinaw City, Mich. The Coffinberry News Bulletin, Vol. VII, No. 8. Wright L. Coffinberry Chapter, Michigan Archaeological Society, Grand Rapids, Sept., 1960, pp. 93-97, 100, 4 illus.

214. —— . Flaked Implements. The Coffinberry News Bulletin, Vol. VII, No. 9. Wright L. Coffinberry Chapter, Michigan Archaeological Society, Grand Rapids, Oct., 1960, p. 111, 1 illus.

215. —— . The Flat River Site No. 26, Kent Co., Mich. The Coffinberry News Bulletin, Vol. VII, No. 10. Wright L. Coffinberry Chapter, Michigan Archaeological Society, Grand Rapids, Nov., 1960, pp. 116-119, 2 illus.

216. Gillis, E[dward] V. Hopewell Culture Artifacts, Brooks Component—Newaygo Co., Mich. The Coffinberry News Bulletin, Vol. VII, No. 11. Wright L. Coffinberry Chapter, Michigan Archaeological Society, Grand Rapids, Dec., 1960, pp. 131-135, 8 illus.

217. [Gillis, Edward V.], editor. Birdstone Find. The Coffinberry News Bulletin, Vol. VIII, No. 1. Wright L. Coffinberry Chapter, Michigan Archaeological Society, Grand Rapids, Jan., 1961, pp. 9-10, 12, 1 illus.

Locates and illustrates a birdstone found near Mud Lake, Berrien County.

218. —— . Manistee Site No. RB-1. The Coffinberry News Bulletin, Vol. VIII, No. 1. Wright L. Coffinberry Chapter, Michigan Archaeological Society, Grand Rapids, Jan., 1961, pp. 10-12, 2 illus.

219. —— . Manistee Site No. RB-2. The Coffinberry News Bulletin, Vol. VIII, No. 2. Wright L. Coffinberry Chapter, Michigan Archaeological Society, Grand Rapids, Feb., 1961, pp. 17-18, 24, 2 illus.

220. —— . Copper Spear Head, Socketed Type. The Coffinberry News Bulletin, Vol. VIII, No. 3. Wright L. Coffinberry Chapter, Michigan Archaeological Society, Grand Rapids, March, 1961, pp. 32-33, 1 illus.

Includes the illustration of a copper artifact found on the surface in Troy Township, Newaygo County.

221. —— . Rim Sherds—Owasco Culture. The Coffinberry News Bulletin, Vol. VIII, No. 3. Wright L. Coffinberry Chapter, Michigan Archaeological Society, Grand Rapids, March, 1961, p. 36, 1 illus.

Rim sherds found at Butler Site, Dearborn, Wayne County, illustrated.

222. Gillis, E[dward] V. Crockery Creek Site—Field Trip Report. The Coffinberry News Bulletin, Vol. VIII, No. 5. Wright L. Coffinberry Chapter, Michigan Archaeological Society, Grand Rapids, May, 1961, pp. 61-62, 64, 1 illus.

223. [Gillis, Edward V.], editor. Site Reports. The Coffinberry News Bulletin, Vol. VIII, No. 6. Wright L. Coffinberry Chapter, Michigan Archaeological Society, Grand Rapids, June, 1961, pp. 74-77, 2 illus.

Reprint of article of entry No. 279.

224. ——— . Unusual Pottery Find. The Coffinberry News Bulletin, Vol. VIII, No. 6. Wright L. Coffinberry Chapter, Michigan Archaeological Society, Grand Rapids, June, 1961, pp. 79-80, 1 illus.

Photographic illustration in full size of a complete pot found in Ottawa County in 1960.

225. ——— . The Coffinberry News Bulletin, Vol. VIII, No. 7. Wright L. Coffinberry Chapter, Michigan Archaeological Society, Grand Rapids, July-Aug., 1961, p. 92, 1 illus.

Illustrates in full size a notched gorget and a projectile point found in Newaygo and Montcalm Counties, respectively.

226. Gillis, E[dward] V. A Progress Report on Archeological Excavations at Fort Michilimackinac, Mackinaw City, Mich., 1961 Field Season. The Coffinberry News Bulletin, Vol. VIII, No. 8. Wright L. Coffinberry Chapter, Michigan Archaeological Society, Grand Rapids, Sept., 1961, pp. 104-108, 2 illus.

227. [Gillis, Edward V.], editor. The Coffinberry News Bulletin, Vol. VIII, No. 10, Wright L. Coffinberry Chapter, Michigan Archaeological Society, Grand Rapids, Nov., 1961, p. 133, 1 illus.

Full-size illustration of a celt, spear point and a horn-like object found on surface near Casnovia.

228. ——— . A Recent Copper Find. The Coffinberry News Bulletin, Vol. VIII, No. 11. Wright L. Coffinberry Chapter, Michigan Archaeological Society, Grand Rapids, Dec., 1961, p. 146, 1 illus.

A Wexford County copper projectile point found in 1961 illustrated in full size.

229. ——— . A Ft. Michilimackinac Excavation Highlight. The Coffinberry News Bulletin, Vol. VIII, No. 11. Wright L. Coffinberry Chapter, Michigan Archaeological Society, Grand Rapids, Dec., 1961, pp. 146-47, 2 illus.

Description and drawing of a well found at the fort.

230. ——— . Archeology in "The Good Old Days." The Coffinberry News Bulletin, Vol. IX, No. 1. Wright L. Coffinberry Chapter, Michigan Archaeological Society, Grand Rapids, Jan., 1962, pp. 3-5.

Excerpts from the minutes of Kent Scientific Institute of 1875. Taken from report on mound explorations in Lamont and on Deer Creek. Shape and dimensions given for latter mound.

231. ——— . A Soaper [sic] Stone? The Coffinberry News Bulletin, Vol. IX, No. 4. Wright L. Coffinberry Chapter, Michigan Archaeological Society, Grand Rapids, April, 1962, p. 46, 1 illus.

232. Gillis, E[dward] V. Engraved Celt. The Coffinberry News Bulletin, Vol. IX, No. 5. Wright L. Coffinberry Chapter, Michigan Archaeological Society, Grand Rapids, May, 1962, pp. 50-54, 1 illus.

Additional information on artifact in above article. See Soper (Index).

233. [Gillis, Edward V.,] editor. The Paw-Paw Lake Stone. The Coffinberry News Bulletin, Vol. IX, No. 6. Wright L. Coffinberry Chapter, Michigan Archaeological Society, Grand Rapids, June, 1962, pp. 64-65, 1 illus.

234. Gillis, E[dward] V. Recent Indian Burial Find at Grandville, Mich. The Coffinberry News Bulletin, Vol. IX, No. 6. Wright L. Coffinberry Chapter, Michigan Archaeological Society, Grand Rapids, June, 1962, pp. 68-74, 3 illus.

235. [Gillis, Edward V.,] editor. Black Flint Projectile Points. The Coffinberry News Bulletin, Vol. IX, No. 7. Wright L. Coffinberry Chapter, Michigan Archaeological Society, Grand Rapids, July-Aug., 1962, pp. 83-85, 2 illus.

236. ——— . A Brief Recap on University of Michigan Fieldwork, 1962. The Coffinberry News Bulletin, Vol. IX, No. 10. Wright L. Coffinberry Chapter, Michigan Archaeological Society, Grand Rapids, Nov., 1962, pp. 113-114.

237. ——— . A Miniature Clay Pipe. The Coffinberry News Bulletin, Vol. IX, No. 11. Wright L. Coffinberry Chapter, Michigan Archaeological Society, Grand Rapids, Dec., 1962, p. 125, 1 illus.

238. Gil[l]man, Henry. The Flattest Tibia on Record. The American Naturalist, Vol. V., No. 10. Peabody Academy of Science, Salem, Mass., Oct., 1871, pp. 663-664.

239. ——— . Explorations on the St. Clair River, Michigan. Sixth Annual Report, Peabody Museum of American Archaeology and Ethnology, Vol. I. Harvard College, Cambridge, Mass., 1873, pp. 13-19.

See entry No. 245.

240. ——— . Ancient Works at Isle Royale, Michigan. Appletons' Journal of Literature, Science, and Arts, Vol. X, No. 229. New York, D. Appleton & Co., Aug., 1873, pp. 173-175.

241. Gillman, Henry. The Mound-Builders and Platycnemism in Michigan. Annual Report, Smithsonian Institution, 1873. Washington, D. C., Government Printing Office, 1874, pp. 364-390, 3 illus., 9 maps.

242. ——— . Perforation of the Humerus Conjoined with Platycnemism. The American Naturalist, Vol. IX, No. 7. Salem, Mass., Peabody Academy of Science, 1875, pp. 427-428.

243. —— . The Ancient Men of the Great Lakes. [abstract.] Proceedings of the American Association for the Advancement of Science, 24th Meeting, Held at Detroit, Michigan, August 1875. Published by the Permanent Secretary, Salem, Mass., 1876, pp. 316-322.

244. —— . Certain Characteristics Pertaining to Ancient Man in Michigan. Annual Report, Smithsonian Institution, 1875. Washington, D. C., Government Printing Office, 1876, pp. 234-245, 13 illus.

245. —— . Explorations on the St. Clair River, Michigan. Reports of the Peabody Museum of American Archaeology and Ethnology, Harvard University, Vol. I, 1868-1876. Printed by order of the Board of Trustees, Cambridge, Mass., 1876, pp. 13-19.

> Henry Gillman given an appropriation by the Trustees to conduct exploration of several mounds at head of St. Clair River. Artifacts recovered and Gillman report received by Museum. Five mounds excavated, several others tested. See entry No. 239.

246. —— . Peculiarities of the Femora from Tumuli in Michigan. Proceedings of the American Association for the Advancement of Science, 25th Meeting, Held at Buffalo, N. Y., August 1876. Published by the Permanent Secretary, Salem, Mass., 1877, pp. 300-307.

247. —— . Some Observations on the Orbits of the Mound Crania. Proceedings of the American Association for the Advancement of Science, 25th Meeting, Held at Buffalo, N. Y., August 1876. Published by the Permanent Secretary, Salem, Mass., 1877, pp. 307-311.

248. Investigation of the Burial Mound at Fort Wayne, on the Detroit River, Michigan. Proceedings of the American Association for the Advancement of Science, 25th Meeting, Held at Buffalo, N. Y., August 1876. Published by the Permanent Secretary, Salem, Mass., 1877, pp. 311-325.

249. —— . Les Témoignages Ostéologiques Fournis par les Anciens Mounds du Michigan. Congrès International des Américanistes (Luxembourg, 1877), Vol. I, Seconde Session, Nancy, France. Printed by Libraire Luxembourg, Paris Editeurs, 1878, pp. 64-77.

250. —— . Additional Facts Concerning Artificial Perforation of the Cranium in Ancient Mounds in Michigan. Proceedings of the American Association for the Advancement of Science, 26th Meeting, Held at Nashville, Tenn., August 1877. Published by the Permanent Secretary, Salem, Mass., 1878, pp. 335-339.

251. —— . The Mound-Builders in Michigan. Michigan Pioneer and Historical Collections, Vol. II. Detroit, Wm. Graham's Presses, 1880, pp. 40-52.

252. —— . Further Confirmation of the Post-Mortem Character of the Cranial Perforation from Michigan Mounds. The American Naturalist, Vol. XIX, No. 11. Philadelphia, McCalla & Stavely, Nov., 1885, pp. 1127-1128.

253. ——. The Mound-Builders in Michigan. Michigan Pioneer and Historical Collections, Vol. III. Lansing, Robert Smith Printing Co., 1903, pp. 202-213.

254. ——. Investigation of the Burial Mound at Fort Wayne, on the Detroit River, Michigan. The Totem Pole, Vol. XIII, No. 6. Aboriginal Research Club, Detroit, Sept., 1944, pp. 1-7.

Reprint of entry No. 248.

255. ——. The Tuetelos. The Totem Pole, Vol. XXX, No. 1. Aboriginal Research Club, Detroit, Mich., Oct., 1952, pp. 1-2.

Mounds along Detroit River ascribed to Tuetelos Indians.

256. ——. Investigation of the Burial Mound at Fort Wayne, on the Detroit River, Michigan. Michigan Archaeologist, Vol. IV, No. 3. Michigan Archaeological Society, Ann Arbor, Sept., 1958, pp. 56-68, 1 illus.

Reprint of entry No. 248. Tables and interpretation of statistics left out because now invalid.

257. ——. Burial Mounds Near Fort Wayne, Detroit. Michigan Archaeologist, Vol. IV, No. 4. Michigan Archaeological Society, Ann Arbor, Dec., 1958, pp. 71-73.

Partial reprint, under new title, of entry No. 241.

258. Goss, Dwight. History of Grand Rapids and Its Industries. 2 Vols. Chicago, C. F. Cooper and Co., 1906. Vol. I, Chap. 1, "Prehistoric Grand Rapids," pp. 9-35.

259. Green, Amos R. Fluted Points and Archaic Relationships in the Midwest. Unpublished manuscript, presented in 1952 at the Society of American Archaeology Round Table on the Paleo-Indian of the Eastern United States and Arctic Regions, and on file at the Pennsylvania State Museum, Harrisburg, Pa.

260. ——. Michigan Archaeological Society News, Vol. I, No. 4. Michigan Archaeological Society, Ann Arbor, Oct., 1954, pp. 1-3, 1 illus.

Tells of the survey and exploratory work on an earthwork enclosure near Summerville, Pokagon Township, Cass County.

261. ——. The Archaeological Survey of the Muskegon Pipeline. Service Pipeline Company, 1958 (second printing), pp. 25, 9 illus.

262. ——. An Adena Type Gorget in Michigan. Michigan Archaeologist, Vol. VII, No. 3. Michigan Archaeological Society, Ann Arbor, Sept., 1961, pp. 30-31, 1 illus.

263. Greenman, E[merson] F. A Report on Michigan Archaeology. American Anthropologist, N.S., Vol. XXVIII, No. 1. Menasha, Wis., George Banta Publishing Co., 1926, pp. 310-313.

Reviews status of Michigan archaeology up to 1926 and presents archaeological problems that need to be investigated.

264. ——. Michigan Mounds, with Special Reference to Two in Missaukee County. Papers of the Michigan Academy of Science, Arts, and Letters, Vol. VII. New York, The Macmillan Co., 1927, pp. 1-9.

265. ——. The Archaeological Collection in the Michigan Pioneer Museum. Michigan History Magazine, Vol. XII, No. 2. Michigan Historical Commission, Lansing, 1928, pp. 350-376.

266. ——. With appendices by Frederick R. Matson, Jr., and Byron O. Hughes, The Younge Site: An Archaeological Record from Michigan. Occasional Contributions from the Museum of Anthropology of the University of Michigan, No. 6. Ann Arbor, University of Michigan, 1937, pp. 172, 33 illus., 9 tabs., 10 maps.

267. ——. Extracts from Dr. Greenman's Letter. The Totem Pole, Vol. I, No. 2. Aboriginal Research Club, Detroit, Mich., May, 1938, 2 unnumbered pp.

Statement of conditions under which Greenman agrees to direct excavations at Gibraltar site, equipment needed, purpose of the work.

268. ——. Cultural Relationships of Archaeological Sites in the Upper Great Lakes Region. Papers of the Michigan Academy of Science, Arts, and Letters, Vol. XXIV, Pt. 4. Ann Arbor, University of Michigan Press, 1939, pp. 1-10.

269. ——. System in Cataloguing Artifacts. The Totem Pole, Vol. III, No. 4. Aboriginal Research Club, Detroit, Mich., July, 1939, pp. 1-3, 2 illus.

270. ——. The Wolf and Furton Sites, Macomb County, Michigan. Occasional Contributions from the Museum of Anthropology of the University of Michigan, No. 8. Ann Arbor, University of Michigan, 1939, pp. 34, 12 illus., 4 maps.

271. ——. The Hopewellian in the Detroit-Windsor Area. Papers of the Michigan Academy of Science, Arts, and Letters, Vol. XXX, Pt. 4, Ann Arbor, University of Michigan Press, 1945, pp. 457-464, 2 illus.

272. ——. A Jar Showing Clay Slip in the Southeastern Michigan Woodland Pattern. Papers of the Michigan Academy of Science, Arts, and Letters, Vol. XXXIII, Pt. 4. Ann Arbor, University of Michigan Press, 1949, pp. 255-257, 1 illus.

273. ——. Discussion of Great Lakes Prehistory at the Christmas Meeting of the American Anthropological Association in Detroit. Michigan Archaeological Society News, Vol. II, No. 1. Michigan Archaeological Society, Ann Arbor, Jan., 1955, pp. 1-4.

274. ——. The Woodland Culture in Michigan. Michigan Archaeological Society News, Vol. II, No. 3. Michigan Archaeological Society, Ann Arbor, Aug., 1956, pp. 7-12, 5 illus.

275. ——. An American Eolithic? American Antiquity, Vol. XXII, No. 3. Society for American Archaeology, Salt Lake City, Utah, Jan., 1957, p. 298.

276. ——. Not Yet Gone, But Going. Michigan Archaeologist, Vol. III, No. 1. Michigan Archaeological Society, Ann Arbor, March, 1957, pp. 1-2.

An editorial on Michigan archaeological remains, including a description of rock carvings in the Upper and Lower Peninsula.

277. ——. Riviere au Vase Site. Michigan Archaeologist, Vol. III, No. 1. Michigan Archaeological Society, Ann Arbor, March, 1957, pp. 9-11.

See entry No. 308 for the pottery report of this site.

278. ——. The Garden Beds Around Lake Michigan. Michigan Archaeologist, Vol. III, No. 2. Michigan Archaeological Society, Ann Arbor, June, 1957, pp. 12-27, 4 illus.

279. ——. The Designation of Archaeological Sites in Michigan. Michigan Archaeologist, Vol. III, No. 4. Michigan Archaeological Society, Ann Arbor, Dec., 1957, pp. 87-93, 3 illus.

280. ——. An Early Historic Cemetery at St. Ignace. Michigan Archaeologist, Vol. IV, No. 2. Michigan Archaeological Society, Ann Arbor, July, 1958, pp. 28-35.

281. ——. Prehistoric Detroit. Michigan Archaeologist, Vol. IV, No. 4. Michigan Archaeological Society, Ann Arbor, Dec., 1958, pp. 81-93, 3 illus.

282. ——. A Prehistoric Hunting-Knife from Bay County. Michigan Archaeologist, Vol. VII, No. 1. Michigan Archaeological Society, Ann Arbor, March, 1961, pp. 4-5, 1 illus.

283. Greenman, E. F., J. B. Griffin, and A. C. Spaulding. Notes on the Prehistory of the Upper Great Lakes Area. Friends of the Pleistocene Annual Meeting, 1956, pp. 30-33.

284. Gregory, W. M. Geological Report on Arenac County. Michigan Geological and Biological Survey, Publication 11, Geological Series 8. Published as part of the Annual Report of the Board of Geological and Biological Survey for 1911. Lansing, Wynkoop Hallenbeck Crawford Co., 1912, p.1.

Includes brief statement of indications and locations of camp sites, earthworks, workshops, and burial grounds.

285. Greusel, Joseph. Discussion of the Paper of Hon. David E. Heineman on Local History. Michigan Pioneer and Historical Collections, Vol. XXXV, Pt. I. Lansing, Wynkoop Hallenbeck Crawford Co., 1907, pp. 324-326.

Describes the discovery of Indian copper mine and a 5000 pound copper mass exposed by Indians; also cartloads of aboriginal tools. Discusses skeletal remains, pottery, copper, and other artifacts found in Springwells area.

286. Griffin, James B. An Interpretation of the Glacial Kame Culture. Appendix *In* Occasional Contributions from the Museum of Anthropology of the University of Michigan, No. 12. Ann Arbor, University of Michigan Press, 1948, pp. 46-51.

287. ——, editor. Essays on Archaeological Methods. Anthropological Papers, Museum of Anthropology, University of Michigan, No. 8. Ann Arbor, University of Michigan Press, 1951, pp. 151.

288. ——. The Reliability of Radiocarbon Dates for Late Glacial and Recent Times in Central and Eastern North America. Anthropological Papers, University of Utah, Department of Anthropology, No. 26. Salt Lake City, University of Utah Press, Dec., 1956, pp. 10-34, 2 maps.

289. ——, editor. Lake Superior Copper and the Indians: Miscellaneous Studies of Great Lakes Prehistory. Anthropological Papers, No. 17, Museum of Anthropology, University of Michigan, Ann Arbor, The University of Michigan, 1961, pp. 189, 33 illus., 16 tables, 5 maps.

290. Griffin, James B., and George I. Quimby. Prehistoric Copper Pits on the Eastern Side of Lake Superior. *In* Griffin, James B., Editor, Lake Superior Copper and the Indians, Anthropological Papers, No. 17, Museum of Anthropology, University of Michigan. Ann Arbor, The University of Michigan, 1961, pp. 77-82.

291. Griffin, Leonard. Report on Excavations of a Site at Newburg, Shiawassee County. Michigan Archaeologist, Vol. VII, No. 1. Michigan Archaeological Society, Ann Arbor, March, 1961, pp. 1-3, 1 illus.

292. ——. The Root Site. The Coffinberry News Bulletin, Vol. VIII, No. 11. Wright L. Coffinberry Chapter, Michigan Archaeological Society, Grand Rapids, Dec., 1961, pp. 136-138, 1 illus.

293. ——. American Archaeology for the Amateur. Michigan State University, Oakland, Rochester, Mich., 1962, pp. 64.

A manual for the amateur with a survey of American archaeology that includes Michigan. Revised and republished in 1963 as, "A Handbook for the Amateur Archaeologist," Oakland University, Division of Continuing Education. Illustrated.

294. ——. An Interim Report on the Root Site. Michigan Archaeologist, Vol. VIII, No. 2. Michigan Archaeological Society, Ann Arbor, June, 1962, pp. 11-15, 2 illus.

295. Grogitsky, Norman. Cache. The Totem Pole, Vol. XLII, No. 8. Aboriginal Research Club, Detroit, Mich., Nov., 1959, 1 p., 1 illus.

296. ——. A Pit Burial in Wayne County, Michigan. The Totem Pole, Vol. XLV, No. 4. Aboriginal Research Club, Detroit, April, 1962, 1 p.

297. ——. A Wayne County, Michigan, Bundle Burial. The Totem Pole, Vol. XLV, No. 7. Aboriginal Research Club, Detroit, Oct., 1962, 2 pp., 2 illus.

298. Guthe, Carl E. Archaeology at Our Doorstep. The Michigan Alumnus, Vol. XXXIX, No. 6. Alumni Association of the University of Michigan, Ann Arbor, Nov., 1932, pp. 91-92.

299. ——. Archaeological Fieldwork in North America During 1934. American Antiquity, Vol. I, No. 2, Pt. 2. The Society for American Archaeology, Menasha, Wis., Oct., 1935, pp. 113-114.

## H

300. Hagar, Albert D. Ancient Mining on the Shores of Lake Superior. The Atlantic Monthly, Vol. XV, No. 89. Boston, Mass., Ticknor & Fields, March, 1865, pp. 308-315.

An account of the discovery of the first Indian copper mine near Ontonagon in 1848.

301. Haines, Blanche M. French and Indian Footprints at Three Rivers on the St. Joseph. Michigan Pioneer and Historical Collections, Vol. XXXVIII. Lansing, Wynkoop Hallenbeck Crawford Co., 1912, pp. 386-397, 2 illus.

Includes a description of David C. Beerstecher's excavation of burials and other archaeological features at Three Rivers in 1905-1908. Skeletal remains and artifacts found are illustrated.

302. Haltiner, Gerald. Copper Relics of Northeastern Michigan. The Totem Pole, Vol. XIII, No. 3. Aboriginal Research Club, Detroit, Mich., June, 1944, pp. 1-2.

303. ——. Mr. Haltiner Reports. The Totem Pole, Vol. XV, No. 2. Aboriginal Research Club, Detroit, Mich., May, 1945, pp. 1-2.

Report of the finding of a complete pot and a copper cache on north bank and near the mouth of Thunder Bay River.

304. ——. The Enigma of Morris Bay. The Totem Pole, Vol. XVIII, No. 1. Aboriginal Research Club, Detroit, Mich., Oct., 1946, pp. 1-4, 1 illus.

Locates and describes a boulder fort and its features in Alpena Township, Alpena County.

305. Hard, Robert. Lake Bottom and Bog Aspects of Primitive Culture in Michigan. Michigan Archaeological Society News, Vol. I, No. 3. Michigan Archaeological Society, Ann Arbor, June, 1954, pp. 10-12.

306. ——. A Salvaged Site in Genesee County. Michigan Archaeologist, Vol. VI, No. 1. Michigan Archaeological Society, Grand Rapids, March, 1960, pp. 1-5, 1 illus., 1 map.

307. Harp, Elmer, Jr., compiler. Notes and News. American Antiquity, Vol. XXII, No. 4. Society for American Archaeology, Salt Lake City, Utah, April, 1957, pp. 436-437.

Contains a summary of the results of archaeological field work of The University of Michigan at an Upper Peninsula Old Copper Culture site.

308. Harper, Victoria G. A Ceramic Study of the Riviere au Vase Site in Southeastern Michigan. Papers of the Michigan Academy of Science, Arts, and Letters, Vol. XXX, Pt. 4. Ann Arbor, University of Michigan Press, 1945, pp. 479-491.

See entry No. 277.

309. Hatt, Robert T. Introduction. The Sanilac Petroglyphs, Bull. XXXVI. Cranbrook Institute of Science, Bloomfield Hills, Mich., 1958, pp. 5-20, 12 illus., 2 maps.

310. Herrick, Ruth. A Preliminary Report on the Ada Site. Michigan Archaeological Society News, Vol. II, No. 4. Michigan Archaeological Society, Ann Arbor, Dec., 1956, pp. 7-11.

311. ——— . Report on a Burial in Montcalm County. Michigan Archaeologist, Vol. III, No. 1. Michigan Archaeological Society, Ann Arbor, March, 1957, pp. 8-9.

A burial of the middle 18th century described.

312. ——— . A Report on the Ada Site, Kent County, Michigan. Michigan Archaeologist, Vol. IV, No. 1. Michigan Archaeological Society, Ann Arbor, March, 1958, pp. 1-27, 5 illus, 1 map.

313. Hills, Leslie W. [letter to editor]. The American Archaeologist, Vol. II, Pt. 3. Columbus, O., The Landon Printing and Publishing Co., March 1898, p. 77, 1 illus.

Illustrates and tells of the discovery of a cache of flints and a stone axe found at Moccasin Bluff, Buchanan, Berrien County.

314. Hinsdale, W[ilbert] B. The Missaukee Preserve and Rifle River Forts. Papers of the Michigan Academy of Science, Arts, and Letters, Vol. IV, Pt. 1. New York, The Macmillan Co., 1925, pp. 1-11.

315. ——— . Primitive Man in Michigan. Michigan Handbook Series, No. 1. Ann Arbor, University of Michigan, 1925, pp. 195, 41 illus.

316. ——— . An Unusual Trephined Skull from Michigan. Papers of the Michigan Academy of Science, Arts, and Letters, Vol. IV, Pt. 1. New York, The Macmillan Co., 1925, pp. 13-14, 1 illus.

317. ——— . Archaeological Work by State Agencies, 1925. American Anthropologist, N.S., Vol. XXVIII, No. 4. Menasha, Wis., George Banta Publishing Co., 1926, pp. 681-682.

318. ——— . Archaeological Field Work in North America During 1926, Michigan. American Anthropologist, N.S., Vol. XXIX, No. 2. Menasha, Wis., George Banta Publishing Co., 1927, pp. 316-317.

319. ——— . The Indians of Washtenaw County, Michigan. Ann Arbor, Mich., George Wahr, 1927, pp. 68, 11 illus., 1 map.

320. ——— . Indian Corn Culture in Michigan. Papers of the Michigan Academy of Science, Arts, and Letters, Vol. VIII. New York, The Macmillan Co., 1928, pp. 31-49, 1 illus.

321. ——— . Reports. American Anthropologist, N.S., Vol. XXX, No. 3. Menasha, Wis., George Banta Publishing Co., 1928, pp. 509-511.

Report of archaeological work being done by the University of Michigan.

322. ——. Archaeological Field Work in North America During 1928. American Anthropologist, N.S., Vol. XXXI, No. 2., Menasha, Wis., George Banta Publishing Co., Jan.-March, 1929, pp. 348-349.

Similar report to entry No. 321.

323. ——. Indian Mounds, West Twin Lake, Montmorency County, Michigan. Papers of the Michigan Academy of Science, Arts, and Letters, Vol. X. Ann Arbor, University of Michigan Press, 1929, pp. 91-101, 8 illus., 1 tab.

324. ——. Reports of Archaeological Field Work in the Summer of 1928 in Montmorency, Newaygo and Lake Counties, Michigan. Papers of the Michigan Academy of Science, Arts, and Letters, Vol. XII. Ann Arbor, University of Michigan Press, 1930, pp. 127-135, 6 illus., 1 map.

325. ——. Archaeological Atlas of Michigan. Michigan Handbook Series, #4. Ann Arbor, University of Michigan Press, 1931, pp. 40, 21 illus., 20 maps.

326. ——. Spirit Stones. Papers of The Michigan Academy of Science, Arts, and Letters, Vol. XIV. Ann Arbor, University of Michigan Press, 1931, pp. 103-112.

Locates and briefly describes Michigan spirit stones.

327. ——. Distribution of the Aboriginal Population of Michigan. Occasional Contributions from the Museum of Anthropology of the University of Michigan, No. 2. Ann Arbor, University of Michigan, 1932, pp. 35, 1 illus.

328. ——. Perforated Skulls, An Inquiry. The Wisconsin Archeologist, N.S., Vol. XIV, No. 2. Wisconsin Archeological Society, Milwaukee, Wis., Nov., 1934, p. 37, 1 illus.

329. Hinsdale, W. B., and Stephen C. Cappannari. Distribution of Perforated Human Crania in the Western Hemisphere. Papers of the Michigan Academy of Science, Arts, and Letters, Vol. XXVI, Pt. 4. Ann Arbor, University of Michigan Press, 1941, pp. 459-462.

330. Hinsdale, W. B., and Emerson F. Greenman. Perforated Indian Crania in Michigan, Occasional Contributions from the Museum of Anthropology of the University of Michigan, No. 5. Ann Arbor, University of Michigan Press, Aug., 1936, pp. 15, 7 illus., 1 map.

331. Historical Notes. Michigan History Magazine, Vol. IX, No. 1. Michigan Historical Commission, Lansing, 1925, p. 119.

Locates mounds in Van Buren and Cass Counties.

332. Historical Notes. Michigan History Magazine, Vol. XVI, Spring No. Michigan Historical Commission, Lansing, 1932, pp. 244-248, 1 illus.

Reports the donation of Indian artifact collections to the State Historical Society and the city of Hillsdale.

333. History of Bay County, Michigan. Chicago, H. R. Page and Co., 1883. "Monuments of the Past," by W. R. McCormick, pp. 32-33.

Locates and describes some mounds formerly within the limits of, and others outside of, Bay City. Tells of their excavation and contents.

334. History of Macomb County, Michigan. Chicago, M. A. Leeson and Co., 1882. Chap. 10, "Introduction-Archaeological," pp. 133-166.

Contains information on location of forts and mounds and a survey of some by S. L. Andrews in 1859. Other discoveries of skeletons and artifacts discussed.

335. History of Kent County, Michigan. Chicago, Chas. C. Chapman and Co., 1881, pp. 17-20; 125-134.

"History of Michigan," pp. 17-20, has a section on the Mound-Builders; pp. 125-134, "Archaeology," locates and describes mounds and garden beds.

336. History of Muskegon and Ottawa Counties, Michigan. Chicago, H. R. Page and Co., 1882. "Archaeological," pp. 17-18.

Norton Mounds of Grand Rapids and the Spoonville Mound located and described. Also deals with the mound-builders and their remains.

337. History of Saginaw County, Michigan. Chicago, Chas. C. Chapman and Co., 1881. "History of Michigan—Mound Builders," pp. 17-20; "History of Saginaw County—Archaeology," pp. 282-287.

338. History of St. Clair County, Michigan. Chicago, A. T. Andeas, 1883, pp. 142-176.

Under section Topography and Geology, pp. 142-176, is a subsection, "Archaeological," pp. 155-158, and also another subsection, "Mounds of St. Clair County," pp. 158-160. Quotes Henry Gilman and describes mounds on the St. Clair River and tells of archaeological finds at St. Clair.

339. History of St. Joseph County, Michigan. Philadelphia, L. H. Everts and Co., 1877. Chap. 3, "Ancient Garden Beds, Mounds, and Fortifications," pp. 11-14.

340. Hodge, James S. On the Mineral Region of Lake Superior. Proceedings of the American Association for the Advancement of Science, Second Meeting, Held at Cambridge, [Mass.], August, 1849. Boston, Henry Flanders and Co., 1850, pp. 301-308.

Deals with "relics of ancient mining operations," pp. 307-308.

341. Hodgman, Francis. A Prehistoric Fort at Climax. Michigan Pioneer and Historical Collections, Vol. XXXII. Lansing, Robert Smith Printing Co., 1903, pp. 384-386.

342. Hogg, Victor, and Birt Darling. An Indian Burial Site of the Historic Period in Ingham County. Michigan Archaeologist, Vol. V, No. 1. Michigan Archaeological Society, Ann Arbor, March, 1959, pp. 3-7, 1 illus.

343. Holmes, William H. Aboriginal Copper Mines of Isle Royale, Lake Superior. American Anthropologist, N.S., Vol. III, No. 4. New York, G. P. Putnam's Sons, Oct.-Dec., 1901, pp. 684-696, 3 illus.

344. Holmes, W[illiam] H. Aboriginal Pottery of the Eastern United States. Annual Report, Bureau of American Ethnology, 1898-1899, Washington, D. C., Government Printing Office, 1903, pp. 188, 191-192, 193, 1 illus.

Contains several references to Michigan pottery and includes illustrations of five vessels from the state.

345. Holmquist, Carl E. The Fort Wayne Mound. Aboriginal Research Club Bulletin, Aboriginal Research Club, Detroit, Mich., n.d., pp. 1-13.

346. ——. An Interesting Afternoon. The Totem Pole, Vol. IX, No. 2. Aboriginal Research Club, Detroit, Mich., May, 1942, p. 1.

Brief account of surface finds found at a site on Huron River in Wayne County.

347. ——. A Delta County Village and Workshop Site. The Totem Pole, Vol. XXI, No. 5. Aboriginal Research Club, Detroit, Mich., Aug., 1948, pp. 1-3.

348. Hopewell Mounds at Grand Rapids. Michigan Archaeological Society News, Vol. I, No. 1. Michigan Archaeological Society, Ann Arbor, Jan., 1953, pp. 4-5.

Consists of a brief account of the Hopewell culture in Michigan as found at Grand Rapids and Tecumseh.

349. Hough, Jack L. Pleistocene Chronology of the Great Lakes Region. Office of Naval Research, University of Illinois, Urbana, Jan., 1953, pp. 108, 26 illus.

350. Houghton, Jacob. The Ancient Miners of Lake Superior. *In* A. P. Swineford, History and Review of the Copper, Iron, Silver, Slate and Other Material Interests of the Southern Shore of Lake Superior. The Mining Journal, Marquette, Mich., 1876, pp. 78-89.

351. ——. The Ancient Copper Mines of Lake Superior. Report and Collections on the State Historical Society of Wisconsin, Vol. VIII. Madison, Wis., David Atwood, 1879, pp. 140-151.

Same article as entry No. 350 above.

352. Howard, Ruth. Preliminary Report on the Fort Wayne Mound, Detroit, Michigan. Papers of the Michigan Academy of Science, Arts, and Letters, Vol. XXXIV, Pt. 4. Ann Arbor, University of Michigan Press, 1950, pp. 261-266.

353. Hoy, P. R. Fabrication of Ancient Copper Implements. Report and Collections on the State Historical Society of Wisconsin, Vol. VIII. Madison, Wis., David Atwood, 1879, pp. 169-173.

See entry No. 243.

354. Hrebek, Marion L. Restoration of Flakes on a Quartzite Implement. Papers of the Michigan Academy of Science, Arts, and Letters, Vol. XXX, Pt. 4. Ann Arbor, University of Michigan Press, 1945, pp. 493-497, 1 illus.

355. Hruska, Robert J. A Socketed Copper Harpoon. The Wisconsin Archeologist, Vol. XXXVII, No. 2. Milwaukee, Wisconsin Archeological Society, June, 1956, pp. 50-51, 1 illus.

356. Hubbard, Bela. Ancient Garden Beds of Michigan. The American Antiquarian, Vol. I, No. 1. Cleveland, O., Brooks, Schinkel and Co., April, 1878, pp. 1-9, 8 illus.

357. ——. Relics in Michigan. The American Antiquarian, Vol. II, No. 3. Chicago, Jameson and Morse, 1879-80, pp. 233-235.

Includes information on mounds on or near Detroit River and their contents.

358. ——. Ancient Garden Beds of Michigan. Michigan Pioneer and Historical Collections, Vol. II. Detroit, Wm. Graham's Presses, 1880, pp. 21-35, 8 illus.

359. ——. Memorials of a Half-Century. New York, G. P. Putnam's Sons, 1887, pp. 581, 4 illus., 2 maps.

Pp. 201-261, "Mound Builders in Michigan" and "Ancient Garden Beds in Michigan."

360. ——. Ancient Garden Beds of Michigan. The Totem Pole, Vol. XXXIX, No. 4. Aboriginal Research Club, Detroit, Mich., Jan., 1957, six and one-half unnumbered pp., 8 illus.

Reprint from "Memorials of a Half-Century." See entry No. 359.

361. ——. The Great Mound at the Mouth of River Rouge. Michigan Archaeologist, Vol. IV, No. 4. Ann Arbor, Michigan Archaeological Society, Dec., 1958, pp. 75-81.

362. Hughes, Byron O. Appendix B: Human Remains. *In* The Younge Site, E. F. Greenman, Occasional Contributions from the Museum of Anthropology of the University of Michigan, No. 6. Ann Arbor, University of Michigan 1937, pp. 125-172, 26 tabs.

363. Hulbert, Archer Butler. The Message of the Mound Builders to the Twentieth Century. Society of Colonial Wars in the State of Michigan, 16th Annual Dinner, May 7, 1913. Published by the Society, Detroit, 1913, pp. 17, 1 map.

## I

364. Incomplete Burials. The Totem Pole, Vol. XXIV, No. 3. Aboriginal Research Club, Detroit, Mich., Dec., 1949, pp. 3-4.

A brief account of an incomplete skeleton, lacking skull and long bones, found in Macomb County. Also reports a bundle burial containing a perforated skull, found at Algonac.

## J

365. Jackson, Charles T. Report on the Geological and Mineralogical Survey of the Mineral Lands of the United States in the State of Michigan. Executive Document No. 1, Senate, Vol. III, Pt. 3. Washington, D. C., 1849, pp. 371-935.

Includes a brief account of ancient mining operations in the Lake Superior region, p. 373.

366. Jamison, James K. Red Metal. The Wisconsin Archeologist, N.S., Vol. X, No. 2. Milwaukee, Wisconsin Archeological Society, Jan., 1931, pp. 69-71.

A reprint on the discovery of copper in Ontonagon County, from a pamphlet, "Red Metal," published by same author in 1930.

367. ——. This Ontonagon Country. Ontonagon, Mich., The Ontonagon Herald Co., 1939, "This Historic Pebble," pp. 28-50.

Complete story of the Ontonagon boulder.

368. ——. This Ontonagon Country. 3d ed., Ontonagon, Mich., The Ontonagon Herald, 1948, "The Historic Pebble," pp. 56-74.

369. Jastrow, Morris, Jr. Archaeological Forgeries at Wyman, Michigan. The Nation, Vol. LIV, No. 1387. New York, The Evening Post Publishing Co., Jan., 1892, pp. 71-72.

Refers to the Soper "finds." See Index.

370. Jelinek, Arthur J. A Late Historic Burial from Berrien County. Michigan Archaeologist, Vol. IV, No. 3. Michigan Archaeological Society, Ann Arbor, Sept., 1958, pp. 48-51, 1 illus.

371. Jenks, William Lee. St. Clair County, Michigan, Vol. I. Chicago and New York, Lewis Publishing Co., 1912, Chap. 6, "Our First Families—The Indians," pp. 42-58, 1 map.

This includes a section on "Mound Builders and Mounds," with excerpts on St. Clair County mounds taken from a report by Henry Gillman. See entry No. 245.

372. Johnson, Crisfield. History of Allegan and Barry Counties, Michigan. Philadelphia, D. W. Ensign, 1880. Chap. 2, "Retrospective," pp. 11-14.

Includes information on fortifications, mounds, and garden beds with locations and descriptions.

373. Johnston, LaDow. The Bar Amulet. Bulletin No. 26. Ohio Indian Relic Collectors Society, Columbus, Jan., 1951, pp. 15-18, 1 illus.

Four Michigan bar amulets are illustrated, described, and located.

374. ——. Random Thoughts of LaDow Johnston on Birdstones. Ohio Archaeologist, N.S., Vol. I, No. 1. Ohio Indian Relic Collectors Society, Columbus, April, 1951, 11. 20-26, 1 illus.

Illustrates, locates, and describes eight birdstones from Michigan.

375. ——. Birdstones and Their Distribution Pattern in Ohio. Ohio Archaeologist, N.S., Vol. IV, No. 3. Ohio Indian Relic Collectors Society, Columbus, July, 1954, pp. 8-38, 9 illus.

Illustrates, locates, and describes ten Michigan birdstones of various types.

376. ——. Birdstones and Their Distribution Pattern in Ohio (second installment). Ohio Archaeologist, N.S., Vol. IV, No. 4. Ohio Indian Relic Collectors Society, Columbus, Oct., 1954, pp. 20-36, 5 illus.

Second half of article above. Illustrates, locates, and describes six Michigan birdstones.

## K

377. The Kalamazoo Mound. The Totem Pole, Vol. I, No. 5. Aboriginal Research Club, Detroit, Mich., Aug., 1938, 1 p.

Tells of measurements, excavations, and repair of the Kalamazoo mound. See entry No. 113.

378. Kelsey, Francis W. Archaeological Forgeries at Wyman, Michigan. The Nation, Vol. LIV, No. 1387. New York, The Evening Post Publishing Co., Jan., 1892, p. 71.

Refers to the Soper "finds." See Index.

379. ——. Some Archeological Forgeries from Michigan. American Anthropologist, N.S., Vol. X, No. 1. Lancaster, Pa., New Era Printing Co., Jan.-March, 1908, pp. 48-59, 12 illus.

Refers to the Soper "finds." See Index.

380. ——. A Persistent Forgery. The Nation, Vol. XC, No. 2346, New York, New York Evening Post Co., June, 1910, pp. 603-604.

Refers to Soper "finds." See Index.

381. ——. A Persistent Forgery. The American Antiquarian and Oriental Journal, Vol. XXXIII, No. 1. Benton Harbor, Mich., The Antiquarian Publishing Co., 1911, pp. 26-31.

Refers to Soper "finds." See Index.

382. Kidd, Kenneth E. A Woodland Site Near Chatham, Ontario. Transactions of the Royal Canadian Institute, Vol. XXX, Pt. 2, No. 63. Toronto, Can., Oct., 1954, pp. 141-178.

Compares Michigan and Ontario archaeological cultural associations.

383. Kientz, Phil. Porphyry Axe from Michigan. Ohio Archaeologist, Vol. II, No. 3. Ohio Indian Relic Collectors Society, Columbus, July, 1952, pp. 20-21, 1 illus.

384. Knoblock, Byron W. Banner-Stones of the North American Indian. Published by the author, LaGrange, Ill., 1939, Popular Edition, pp. 596.

Michigan bannerstones in text and illustrations.

385. Kolar, Dav[id] M. Sanilac County Material. The Totem Pole, Vol. XLI, No. 1. Aboriginal Research Club, Detroit, Mich., Jan., 1958, 2 pp., 2 illus.

386. ——. Sanilac County Archaic Site. The Totem Pole, Vol. XLV, No. 1. Aboriginal Research Club, Detroit, Mich., Jan., 1962, 1 p., 1 illus.

387. Kraus, Edward H. Some Unusual Specimens of "Float" Copper. The American Mineralogist, Vol. IX, No. 2. Journal of the Mineralogical Society of America, Menasha, Wis., Feb., 1924, pp. 23-26, 6 illus.

## L

388. Landon, Ray H. The Mining and Fabrication of Copper by the Aborigines of the Lake Superior Region. Minnesota Archaeologist, Vol. VI, No. 2. Minnesota Archaeological Society, Minneapolis, April, 1940, pp. 27-33, 1 illus., 1 map.

389. Lane, Alfred C. Geological Report on Isle Royale, Michigan. Geological Survey of Michigan, Vol. VI, Pt. 1. Lansing, Robert Smith, 1898, pp. 1-26, 45 illus., 1 map.

390. Larson, Robert H. Report on Excavations in Fort Wayne Enclosure. The Totem Pole, Vol. XIII, No. 5. Aboriginal Research Club, Detroit, Mich., Aug., 1944, p. 1.

391. Lathrop, J. H. The Mound-Builders in the Copper Country of Michigan. The Northwest Magazine, Vol. XIX, No. 2. St. Paul, Minn., E. V. Smalley Publishing Co., Feb., 1901, pp. 3-7, 5 illus.

392. ——. Prehistoric Mines of Lake Superior. The American Antiquarian and Oriental Journal, Vol. XXIII, No. 4. Chicago, S. D. Peet, July-Aug., 1901, pp. 249-258, 5 illus.

393. ——. Prehistoric Mines of Lake Superior. *In* Drier, Roy Ward, and Octave Joseph DuTemple, editors. Prehistoric Copper Mining in the Lake Superior Region: A Collection of Reference Articles. Calumet, Mich., Drier and DuTemple, 1961, pp. 119-126.

394. Laut, Jack. Some Midland County Sites. The Totem Pole, Vol. XLIII, No. 6. Aboriginal Research Club, Detroit, Mich., June, 1960. 1 p., 1 illus.

395. Lawton, Charles D. Mines and Mineral Interests of Michigan. The Semi-Centennial of the Admission of the State of Michigan into the Union. Detroit Free Press Printing Co., 1886, pp. 53-77.

A brief review of prehistoric mining is given which includes the discovery of a copper mass at the Mesnard Mine.

396. Leach, M. L. A History of the Grand Traverse Region. Traverse City, Mich., Grand Traverse Herald, 1883, pp. 59.

Locates mounds and earthworks in the Grand Traverse region. A series of newspaper articles bound with a typewritten index at the Michigan State Library, Lansing. Chapter 1 deals with the Mound Builders.

397. ——. Ancient Forts in Ogemaw County, Michigan. Annual Report, Smithsonian Institution, 1884. Washington, D. C., Government Printing Office, 1885, pp. 849-851, 2 maps.

398. ——. Ancient Mounds in Clinton County, Michigan. Annual Report, Smithsonian Institution, 1884. Washington, D. C., Government Printing Office, 1885, pp. 839-848, 1 map.

399. ——. History of the Grand Traverse Region. Michigan Pioneer and Historical Collections, Vol. XXXII. Lansing, Mich., Robert Smith Printing Co., 1903, pp. 14-175.

Reprint of entry No. 396.

400. ——. Ancient Forts in Ogemaw County, Michigan. Michigan Archaeologist, Vol. III, No. 1. Michigan Archaeological Society, Ann Arbor, March, 1957, pp. 22-24.

Reprint of Smithsonian Institution Annual Report for 1884. See entry No. 397.

401. Leechman, Douglas. Bibliography of Harlan I. Smith. 1889-1936. Bulletin No. 112, Annual Reports, National Museum of Canada, 1939-1947. Ottawa, Edmond Cloutier, 1949, pp. 8-14, 1 illus.

402. [Leeson, M. A.] History of Kent County, Michigan. Chicago, Chas. C. Chapman and Co., 1881. "History of Michigan," pp. 17-21, and "Geology, Archaeology, etc.," pp. 117-134.

403. Lewis, T. H. Copper Mines Worked by the Mound Builders. The American Antiquarian and Oriental Journal, Vol. XI, No. 5. Mendon, Ill., S. D. Peet, Sept., 1889, pp. 293-296.

404. List of Additions to the Museum and Library for the Year 1882. Reports of the Peabody Museum of American Archaeology and Ethnology, Harvard University, Vol. III, 1880-1886. Printed by order of the Board of Trustees, Cambridge, Mass., 1887, p. 202.

Records fragments of human crania and other bones, burned clay, worked flint, etc., which were found in mounds on the Detroit River by Henry Gillman, and added to the Museum collections.

405. ——. Reports of the Peabody Museum of American Archaeology and Ethnology, Harvard University, Vol. III, 1880-1886. Printed by order of the Board of Trustees, Cambridge, Mass., 1887, pp. 505 and 508.

Page 505 tells of perforated human crania found in River Rouge mound and presented to Museum by Bela Hubbard. Page 508 lists additions to the Museum's collection which include implements, carved antler, silver, bone, steatite, etc., from a mound in Grand Rapids. Purchased from and given by W. L. Coffinberry and others.

406. List of Additions to the Museum and Library for the Year 1885. 18th and 19th Annual Reports, Peabody Museum of American Archaeology and Ethnology, Vol. III, No. 5 and 6. Cambridge, Mass., Harvard University, 1886, pp. 505, 508.

Reports the presentation of a River Rouge perforated cranium to the museum by Bela Hubbard and of the receipt of a collection of artifacts from the Grand Rapids mounds from Wright L. Coffinberry and others.

407. Little, Henry. Burial Mounds in Michigan. The American Antiquarian, Vol. II, No. 1. Chicago, Jameson and Morse, 1879-1880, pp. 64-65.

Describes burials and grave goods found in a mound near Kalamazoo. Skeleton of an unusually large man found enclosed in a "case" of burned clay.

408. The Little Old Lady of Gibraltar. The Totem Pole, Vol. I, No. 1. Aboriginal Research Club, Detroit, Mich., n.d., three and one-half unnumbered pages.

Report of the burial of a white woman in the Gibraltar Mound, Wayne County, and of artifacts found with her.

## M

409. Manktelow, Chas. W. Michigan (Wexford County) Archaeology. The American Archaeologist, Vol. II, Pt. 4. Columbus, Ohio, The Landon Printing and Publishing Co., April, 1898, pp. 105-106.

410. ——. The American Archaeologist, Vol. II, Pt. 12. Columbus, Ohio, The Landon Printing and Publishing Co., Dec., 1898, p. 323.

Reports mound excavation and finds near Cadillac.

411. ——. Prehistoric Remains of Northern Mich. Popular Science, Vol. XXXVI, No. 11. New York, Science News Co., Nov. 1902, pp. 259-260.

412. Manson, Carl, Howard A. MacCord, and James B. Griffin. The Culture of the Keyser Farm Site. Papers of the Michigan Academy of Science, Arts, and Letters, Vol. XXIX. Ann Arbor, University of Michigan Press, 1944, pp. 375-418, 16 illus., 1 tab.

413. Martin, Paul S., George I. Quimby, and Donald Collier. Indians Before Columbus. Chicago, The University of Chicago Press, 1947, pp. 582.

414. Mason, Ronald J. Two Unusual "Birdstones" from South-Central Michigan. Michigan Archaeologist, Vol. III, No. 1. Michigan Archaeological Society, Ann Arbor, March, 1957, pp. 3-5, 1 illus.

415. ——. Early Man in the Northeast, with Special Reference to Michigan and the Upper Great Lakes Region. Neville Public Museum, Green Bay, Wis., (n.d.) 8 pp, 1 illus., 1 map.

416. ——. Late Pleistocene Geochronology and the Paleo-Indian Penetration into the Lower Michigan Peninsula. Anthropological Papers, No. 11. Museum of Anthropology, University of Michigan. Ann Arbor, University of Michigan, 1958, pp. 48, 12 illus., 5 maps.

417. Mathews, Alfred. History of Cass County, Michigan. Chicago, Waterman, Watkins and Co., 1882. Chap. 1, "Ancient Remains," pp. 11-13.

418. Matson, Frederick R., Jr. Appendix A: Pottery. *In* The Younge Site. Emerson F. Greenman, Occasional Contributions from the Museum of Anthropology of the University of Michigan, No. 6. Ann Arbor, University of Michigan Press, 1937, pp. 99-124, 1 illus, 3 tabs.

419. ——. Further Technological Notes on the Pottery of the Younge Site, Lapeer County, Michigan. Papers of the Michigan Academy of Science, Arts, and Letters, Vol. XXIV, Pt. 4. Ann Arbor, University of Michigan Press, 1939, pp. 11-23, 1 illus.

420. Maxwell, Moreau S., and Lewis H. Binford. Excavation at Fort Michilimackinac, Mackinac City, Michigan, 1959 Season. Cultural Series, Vol. 1, No. 1. Publications of the Museum, Michigan State University, East Lansing, Mich., July, 1961, pp. 130, 33 illus.

421. McCormick, W. R. Mounds and Mound-Builders of the Saginaw Valley. Michigan Pioneer and Historical Collections, Vol. IV. Lansing, Mich., Wynkoop Hallenbeck Crawford Co., 1906, pp. 379-383.

422. McGaugh, Maurice Edron. The Settlement of the Saginaw Basin. Research Paper No. 16, Chap. 1, p. 1-36, Aboriginal Settlement. Chicago, Ill., The University of Chicago, Dec., 1950, 6 maps.

423. McPherron, Alan. The Juntunen Site (20 M K I). The Coffinberry News Bulletin, Vol. IX, No. 3. Wright L. Coffinberry Chapter, Michigan Archaeological Society, Grand Rapids, March, 1962, pp. 30-32.

424. The Michigan State Archeological Society. The Wisconsin Archeologist, N.S., Vol. III, No. 1. Wisconsin Archeological Society, Milwaukee, Wis., Jan., 1924, pp. 26-27.

425. The Michigan State Archeological Survey. The Wisconsin Archeologist, [O.S.], Vol. I, No. 1. Archeological Section of the Wisconsin Natural History Society, Milwaukee, Wis., Oct., 1901, pp. 14-16.

426. Michigan State Archeological Society Notes. Wisconsin Archeologist, N.S., Vol. III, No. 3. Wisconsin Archeological Society, Milwaukee, Wis., July, 1924, pp. 89-90.

Reports such activities as the preparation of archaeological maps; erection of a marker at the Climax, Michigan Indian Fort; and lists some archaeological collections in Michigan.

427. Miles, Suzanne W. A Revaluation of the Old Copper Industry. American Antiquity, Vol. XVI, No. 3. The Society for American Archaeology, Salt Lake City, Utah, 1951, pp. 240-247.

A general paper on the ancient copper industry, including its Michigan aspects.

428. Mills, James Cooke. History of Saginaw County, Michigan. Saginaw, Seeman and Peters, 1918, Vol. I, Chap. 1, "Prehistoric Races," pp. 1-20, 11 illus.

Discusses mounds, earthworks, fortifications, caches, workshops, artifacts, village sites, etc., in Saginaw Valley.

429. Moll, Harold W. New Member Reports on a Folsom Point. The Totem Pole, Vol. XXXV, No. 6. Aboriginal Research Club, Detroit, Mich., March, 1955, pp. 1-2.

Report of the finding of a Folsom-type point near Midland.

430. ——. The Windover Mound. The Totem Pole, Vol. XXXVIII, No. 3. Aboriginal Research Club, Detroit, Mich., June, 1956, pp. 1-4.

431. Moll, Harold W., and Eldon S. Cornelius. Two Prehistoric Lodge Sites Near Midland. Michigan Archaeologist, Vol. III, No. 3. Michigan Archaeological Society, Ann Arbor, Sept., 1957, pp. 57-61, 2 illus.

432. Moll, Harold, and Norman G. Moll. A Short History of the Indian in Midland. *In* Midland, Michigan, Jan., 1954. 8 typewritten pages, 3 pp. of bibliography. M.S. in Michigan State Library, Lansing.

433. —— . Two Late Historic Indian Graves in Midland County. *In* Midland, Michigan, Oct., 1954, 8 typewritten pages, 1 map. Bound with item 432.

434. Moll, Harold W., Norman G. Moll, and Eldon S. Cornelius. Earthwork Enclosures in Ogemaw, Missaukee and Alcona Counties. The Totem Pole, Vol. XLI, No. 3. Aboriginal Research Club, Detroit, Mich., March, 1958, 19 unnumbered pages, 10 illus.

435. Moll, Harold W., and Norman G. Moll. Manito Stones Near Midland. Michigan Archaeologist, Vol. V, No. 4. Michigan Archaeological Society, Grand Rapids, Mich., Dec., 1959, pp. 53-60.

436. Moore, Charles. The Ontonagon Copper Bowlder [sic] in the United States National Museum. Report of the United States National Museum, Smithsonian Institution, 1895. Washington, D. C., Government Printing Office, 1897, pp. 1021-1030, 2 illus.

437. ——. The Ontonagon Boulder in the National Museum at Washington. Michigan Pioneer and Historical Collections, Vol. XXVII. Lansing, Mich., Robert Smith Printing Co., 1897, pp. 260-266.

438. ——. History of Michigan, Vol. I. Chicago, Ill., The Lewis Publishing Co., 1915, pp. 1-19, 4 illus.

Covers the Mound Builders, garden beds, and ancient mining. Includes illustrations of garden beds and the Ontonagon copper boulder *in situ* and on exhibit in the United States National Museum.

439. Moore, W. G. Historical Sketch of Medina Township, Lenawee County, Michigan. Michigan Pioneer and Historical Collections, Vol. XVII, 2d ed. Lansing, Mich., Wynkoop Hallenbeck Crawford Co., 1910, pp. 508-520.

Tells of mounds in villages of Canandaigua and Medina.

440. Moorehead, Warren K. The Stone Age in North America, Vols. I and II. Cambridge, Mass., Houghton Mifflin Co., 1910, p. 312 in Vol. I; pp. 173, 186 in Vol. II;

Michigan barbed axes and copper objects mentioned and illustrated.

441. Mounds and Mound Builders. The Totem Pole, Vol. IX, No. 1. Aboriginal Research Club, Detroit, Mich., April, 1942, pp. 1-3.

Consists of a summary of entry No. 421.

442. Munger, Lynn, and Irvin S. Dougherty. What an Axe. Ohio Archaeologist, Vol. VIII, No. 4. The Archaeological Society of Ohio, Dayton, Oct., 1958, p. 128, 1 illus.

Illustrates a Michigan barbed axe found on Younger Site, Hunters Creek, Lapeer County.

443. Museum of Anthropology. Michigan Archaeological Society News, Vol. II, No. 3. Ann Arbor, Michigan Archaeological Society, Aug., 1956, p. 2.

Reports the discovery of skeletal material exposed by gravel operations near Ford Lake, 14 miles east of Ann Arbor.

## N

444. News of the Chapters. Michigan Archaeological Society News, Vol. I, No. 1. Ann Arbor, Michigan Archaeological Society, Jan., 1953, pp. 1-2.

Tells of the field trips, surveys, excavations, etc., of the Benton Harbor, Lansing, and Southeastern Chapters.

445. ——. Michigan Archaeological Society News, Vol. I, No. 2. Ann Arbor, Michigan Archaeological Society, Jan., 1954, pp. 1-3.

Various chapters report on their field trips, surface finds, excavations, and collections.

446. ——. Michigan Archaeological Society News, Vol. II, No. 2. Ann Arbor, Michigan Archaeological Society, Sept., 1955, pp. 2-3.

Briefly describes a copper collection found in Alpena area.

447. ——. Michigan Archaeological Society News, Vol. II, No. 4. Ann Arbor, Michigan Archaeological Society, Dec., 1956. pp. 1-7.

Various chapters report excavation results.

448. Nichols, Frances S. (compiler). Index to Schoolcraft's "Indian Tribes of the United States." Bureau of American Ethnology, Bulletin 152, Smithsonian Institution. Washington, D. C., U. S. Government Printing Office, 1954, pp. 257.

See entry No. 552.

## O

449. Oakes, H. E. (Pseud. for Harlan I. Smith). The Garden Beds of Michigan Modeled. The American Antiquarian and Oriental Journal, Vol. XVIII, No. 6. Good Hope, Ill., Stephen D. Peet, Nov.-Dec., 1896, p. 323.

450. Other Additions to the Collections. Reports of the Peabody Museum of American Archaeology and Ethnology, Harvard University, Vol. I, 1868-1876. Printed by order of the Board of Trustees, Cambridge, Mass., 1876, p. 26.

Notes the donation by Henry Gillman of human bone and of stone implements from a mound at the head of the St. Clair River; trade silver from the Lake Superior region; human bones from River Rouge mound, etc.

## P

451. Packard, R. L. Pre-Columbian Copper-Mining in North America. Annual Report, Smithsonian Institution, 1891. Washington, D. C., Government Printing Office, 1892, pp. 175-198.

A general review of prehistoric copper mining and the significance of the metal in prehistoric cultures. Michigan mines and artifacts included.

452. ——. Pre-Columbian Copper Mining in North America, Pt. I. The American Antiquarian and Oriental Journal, Vol. XV, No. 2. Chicago, Ill., S. D. Peet, March, 1893, pp. 67-78.

Same article as entry No. 451.

453. ——. Pre-Columbian Copper Mining in North America, Pt. II. The American Antiquarian and Oriental Journal, Vol. XV, No. 3. Chicago, Ill., S. D. Peet, May, 1893, pp. 152-164.

454. ——. The Use of Copper Among the American Indians. Scientific American, Vol. LXIX, No. 19. New York, Munn and Co., Nov., 1893, p. 294.

A summary, under a different title, of the article appearing in above two entries, Nos. 451, 452, and 453.

455. Palmer, Friend. Early Days in Detroit. Detroit, Mich., Hunt and June, 1906. "Remarkable Specimen of Native Copper," pp. 247-253.

An account of the discovery of the Ontonagon copper boulder in the Ontonagon River and its transfer to the U. S. National Museum.

456. Papworth, Mark. The Sanilac County Rock Carvings. Michigan Archaeologist, Vol. III, No. 4. Michigan Archaeological Society, Ann Arbor, Dec., 1957, pp. 83-87.

457. ——. An Archeological Survey of the Petroglyph Site. The Sanilac Petroglyphs, Bull. 36. Cranbrook Institute of Science, Bloomfield Hills, Mich., 1958, pp. 39-45, 3 illus.

Republication, with minor changes and additions, of, "The Sanilac County Rock Carvings," above.

458. ——. Artifacts from the Kimmel Site, Berrien Springs, Michigan. Michigan Archaeologist, Vol. IV, No. 3. Michigan Archaeological Society, Ann Arbor, Sept., 1958, pp. 51-56, 1 illus.

459. ——. Cultural Relations of the Andrews Site, Saginaw County, Michigan. The Coffinberry News Bulletin, Vol. VI, No. 4. Wright L. Coffinberry Chapter, Michigan Archaeological Society, Grand Rapids, Mich., April, 1959, pp. 37-38.

460. Parchert, Karl G. A Brief Description of Some Interesting Remains in Mecosta County, Michigan. The Totem Pole, Vol. XI, No. 1. Aboriginal Research Club, Detroit, Mich., April, 1943, pp. 2-3.

461. ——. Interesting Relics in Mecosta County. The Totem Pole, Vol. XXV, No. 6. Aboriginal Research Club, Detroit, Mich., Sept., 1950, pp. 1-3.

462. ——. Excavation of a Brownstown Township Refuse Pit. The Totem Pole, Vol. XXVIII, No. 1. Aboriginal Research Club, Detroit, Mich., Oct., 1951, pp. 3-5.

463. Parks, Cameron. Birdstones. Ohio Archaeologist, N.S., Vol. I, No. 3. Ohio Indian Relic Collectors Society, Columbus, Oct., 1951, p. 34, 2 illus.

Illustrates and locates the place where three birdstones were found in Michigan.

464. Peet, Stephen D. Agricultural and Emblematic Works in America. The American Antiquarian and Oriental Journal, Vol. VII, No. 1. Chicago, F. H. Revell, Jan., 1885, pp. 15-38, 21 illus.

Quotes Bela Hubbard on garden beds of Michigan.

465. ——. Archaeology and Ethnology of Michigan. The American Antiquarian and Oriental Journal, Vol. X, No. 1. Mendon, Ill., S. D. Peet, Jan., 1888, pp. 36-39, 1 illus., 1 map.

466. ——. The Mound Builders: Their Works and Relics, Vol. I. Office of the American Antiquarian, Chicago, Ill. 1892, pp. 35, 349-350.

Ascribes copper mines and garden beds to the Mound-Builders.

467. ——. Prehistoric America: The Mound Builders: Their Works and Relics, 2d ed. Office of the American Antiquarian, Chicago, 1903, p. 340.

468. Peru, Donald V. The Probable Site of a Mide [sic] Lodge Near Evart, Michigan. The Coffinberry News Bulletin, Vol. VIII, No. 9. Wright L. Coffinberry Chapter, Michigan Archaeological Society, Grand Rapids, Oct., 1961, pp. 113-116, 1 illus.

469. Peske, G. Richard. Spoonville Mounds. The Coffinberry News Bulletin, Vol. IX, No. 10. Wright L. Coffinberry Chapter, Michigan Archaeological Society, Grand Rapids, Nov., 1962, p. 119.

470. Phillips, George Brinton. A Prehistoric Copper Mine. The Wisconsin Archeologist, N.S., Vol. II, No. 3. Wisconsin Archeological Society, Milwaukee, Wis., July, 1923, pp. 151-154, 1 illus.

Gives the details of the discovery of a Michigan prehistoric copper mine in 1864.

471. Pierce, H. B. History of Calhoun County, Michigan. Philadelphia, L. H. Everts and Co., 1877, Chap. 3, "Ancient Fortifications, etc.," pp. 11-12.

472. Pilling, Arnold R. Local History and Local Archaeology. Bulletin, Detroit Historical Society, Vol. XVI, No. 1. Detroit Historical Society, Detroit, Mich., Oct., 1959, pp. 4-10, 3 illus., 1 map.

473. ——. Six Archaeological Sites in the Detroit Area I. Michigan Archaeologist, Vol. VII, No. 3. Michigan Archaeological Society, Ann Arbor, Sept., 1961, pp. 13-30.

474. ——. Six Archaeological Sites in the Detroit Area II. Michigan Archaeologist, Vol. VII, No. 4. Michigan Archaeological Society, Ann Arbor, Dec., 1961, pp. 34-54.

475. Pohrt, Richard A. The Iron Trade Axe and Tomahawk in Michigan. Michigan Archaeologist, Vol. III, No. 2. Michigan Archaeological Society, Ann Arbor, June, 1957, pp. 28-31.

476. A Possible Copper Route. The Totem Pole, Vol. XVIII, No. 6. Aboriginal Research Club, Detroit, Mich., March, 1947, pp. 1-4, 1 illus.

Reconstructs the possible routes by which northern Michigan copper was shipped to the east and south.

477. Post, H. D. The Rabbit River Mounds and Circles. Michigan Pioneer and Historical Collections, Vol. III. Lansing, Mich., Robert Smith Printing Co., 1903, pp. 296-298.

478. Pottowattomi Village. The Totem Pole, Vol. XVIII, No. 6. Aboriginal Research Club, Detroit, Mich., March, 1947, p. 6.

Tells of a cemetery formerly located in what is now the city of Detroit. Reprinted from The John Askin Papers. See entry No. 487.

479. Powell, J. W. 9th Annual Report, Bureau of American Ethnology, Smithsonian Institution, 1887-1888. Washington, D. C., U. S. Government Printing Office, 1892, pp. xxv-xxvi.

Tells of mound explorations in Michigan and elsewhere by Cyrus Thomas, Gerard Fowke, James D. Middleton, and Henry L. Reynolds.

480. Powers, Perry F. A History of Northern Michigan and Its People, 2 Vols. Chicago, The Lewis Publishing Co., 1912. Vol. I, Chap. 2, "First Lords of the Soil," pp. 32-53.

Pages 32-34 deal with aboriginal remains in northern Michigan.

481. Praus, Alexis A. The Past Meets the Future in Kalamazoo. Michigan History, Vol. XXXIX, No. 1. Lansing, Michigan Historical Commission, March, 1955, pp. 110-116, 2 illus.

Gives details of the excavation of and findings in the Kalamazoo Bronson Park Mound and the insertion of a "time capsule."

482. ——. Rock Painting, Delta County. Michigan Archaeologist, Vol. VI, No. 1. Grand Rapids, Mich., Michigan Archaeological Society, March, 1960, p. 17.

Brief statement of the condition of a Delta County rock painting.

483. ——, editor. The Kalamazoo Mound: A Letter from Alexander J. Sheldon. Michigan History, Vol. XLIV, No. 4. Lansing, Michigan Historical Commission, Dec., 1960, pp. 384-400.

Review of published information on the Kalamazoo Bronson Park Mound and additional new data as revealed in a heretofore unpublished "letter."

484. Prehistoric Bones Here. Michigan Pioneer and Historical Collections, Vol. XXXV. Lansing, Wynkoop Hallenbeck Crawford Co., 1907, pp. 703-704.

Report on the contents of a mound north of Pentwater which included a buffalo skull.

485. Prehistoric Remains in Michigan. Records of the Past, Vol. III, Pt. 3. Records of the Past Exploration Society, Washington, D. C., March, 1904, pp. 95-96, 1 illus.

486. Proposed Survey of the Antiquities of Michigan. Science, N.S., Vol. XIII, No. 330. New York, The Macmillan Co., April, 1901, p. 672.

Details of a state bill that was referred to the Committee on Ways and Means in 1901.

## Q

487. Quaife, Milo M., editor. The John Askin Papers, Vol. I. Detroit, Mich., Detroit Library Commission, 1928, pp. 46-47, 1 map.

Footnote 27 locates an Indian cemetery and village in vicinity of 21st and 24th streets [1928]. Includes a map of 1768 showing Indian villages on both sides of the Detroit River.

488. Quimby, George I. Notes on Indian Trade Silver Ornaments in Michigan. Papers of the Michigan Academy of Science, Arts, and Letters, Vol. XXII. Ann Arbor, University of Michigan Press, 1937, pp. 15-24, 3 illus., 1 tab.

489. ———. Dated Indian Burials in Michigan. Papers of the Michigan Academy of Science, Arts, and Letters, Vol. XXIII. Ann Arbor, University of Michigan Press, 1938, pp. 63-72, 2 illus.

490. ———. Aboriginal Camp Sites on Isle Royale, Michigan. American Antiquity, Vol. IV, No. 3. Society for American Archaeology, Menasha, Wis., Jan., 1939, pp. 215-223, 2 illus.

491. ———. European Trade Articles as Chronological Indicators for the Archaeology of the Historic Period in Michigan. Papers of the Michigan Academy of Science, Arts, and Letters, Vol. XXIV, Pt. 4. Ann Arbor, University of Michigan Press, 1939, pp. 25-31, 2 illus.

492. ———. Hopewellian Pottery Types in Michigan. Papers of the Michigan Academy of Science, Arts, and Letters, Vol. XXVI. Ann Arbor, University of Michigan Press, 1941, pp. 489-494, 1 illus., 1 tab

493. ———. The Goodall Focus: An Analysis of Ten Hopewellian Components in Michigan and Indiana. Prehistory Research Series, Vol. II, No. 2. Indiana Historical Society, Indianapolis, Oct., 1941, pp. 63-161, 17 illus.

494. ———. Indian Trade Objects in Michigan and Louisiana. Papers of the Michigan Academy of Science, Arts, and Letters, Vol. XXVII. Ann Arbor, University of Michigan Press, 1942, pp. 543-551, 1 illus., 1 tab.

495. ———. The Ceramic Sequence within the Goodall Focus. Papers of the Michigan Academy of Science, Arts, and Letters, Vol. XXVIII. Ann Arbor, University of Michigan Press, 1943, pp. 543-548, 2 illus.

496. ———. Some New Data on the Goodall Focus. Papers of the Michigan Academy of Science, Arts, and Letters, Vol. XXIX. Ann Arbor, University of Michigan Press, 1944, pp. 419-423, 1 illus.

497. ———. The Archeology of the Upper Great Lakes Area. *In* Archeology of Eastern United States, edited by James B. Griffin. Chicago, University of Chicago Press, 1952, pp. 99-107.

498. ———. An Old Copper Site at Menominee, Michigan. The Wisconsin Archeologist, Vol. XXXVIII, No. 2. Wisconsin Archeological Society, Milwaukee, Wis., June, 1957, pp. 37-41, 1 illus.

499. Quimby, George I., and Albert C. Spaulding. The Old Copper Culture and the Keweenaw Waterway. Fieldiana: Anthropology, Vol. XXXVI, No. 8. Chicago Natural History Museum, Nov., 1957, pp. 189-201, 7 illus.

500. Quimby, George I. Fluted Points and Geochronology of the Lake Michigan Basin. American Antiquity, Vol. XXIII, No. 3. The Society for American Archaeology, Salt Lake City, Utah, Jan., 1958, pp. 247-254, 5 illus.

501. ———. Late Archaic Culture and the Algoma Beach in the Lake Michigan Basin. The Wisconsin Archeologist, N.S., Vol. XXXIX, No. 3. The Wisconsin Archeological Society, Milwaukee, Sept., 1958, pp. 175-179, 1 illus.

502. ——. Silver Ornaments and the Indians. Miscellanea Paul Rivet Octogenario Dicata, 31 Congreso Internacional de Americanistas, Vol. 31, Pt. 1. Mexico, D. F., Universidad Nacional Autonoma de Mexico, 1958, pp. 317-337, 2 illus.

503. ——. Upper Lakes Farmers and Artists, 100 B. C. Chicago Natural History Museum Bulletin, Vol. XXIX, No. 3. Chicago, March, 1959, pp. 6-7, 2 illus.

504. ——. Lanceolate Points and Fossil Beaches in the Upper Great Lakes Region, American Antiquity, Vol. XXIV, No. 4, Pt. 1. The Society for American Archaeology, Salt Lake City, Utah, April 1959, pp. 424-426.

505. ——. Indian Life in the Upper Great Lakes 11,000 B. C. to A. D. 1800. Chicago, The University of Chicago Press, 1960, pp. 182, illus.

506. ——. Cord Marking Versus Fabric Impressing of Woodland Pottery. American Antiquity, Vol. XXVI, No. 3. Salt Lake City, University of Utah Press, 1961, pp. 426-428, 1 illus.

507. ——. The Pic River Site. *In* Griffin, James B., Editor. Lake Superior Copper and the Indians. Anthropological Papers, No. 17, Museum of Anthropology, University of Michigan. Ann Arbor, The University of Michigan, 1961, pp. 83-89.

508. Quimby, George I., and James B. Griffin. Various Finds of Copper and Stone Artifacts in the Lake Superior Basin. *In* Griffin, James B., Editor. Lake Superior Copper and the Indians. Anthropological Papers, No. 17. Museum of Anthropology, University of Michigan. Ann Arbor, The University of Michigan, 1961, pp. 103-133.

## R

509. A Rare Copper Axe. The Archaeologist, Vol. III, No. 2. Columbus, Ohio, The Archaeologist Co., Feb., 1895, pp. 75-76.

Locates and describes a copper axe found in Jackson County.

510. Rau, Charles. Report upon the Work in the Department of Archaeology in the U. S. National Museum for the Year Ending June 30, 1886. Report of the U. S. National Museum, Smithsonian Institution for 1886, Pt. 2. Washington, D. C., Government Printing Office, 1889, p. 107.

Records the receipt of a platform pipe found in Berrien County.

511. Records of the Past, Vol. II, Pt. 7. Records of the Past Exploration Society, Washington, D. C., July, 1903, p. 223.

Reports the discovery of a prehistoric mine near Rockland, Ontonagon County.

512. Reeder, John T. Evidences of Prehistoric Man on Lake Superior. Michigan Pioneer and Historical Collections, Vol. XXX. Lansing, Mich., Wynkoop Hallenbeck Crawford, 1906, pp. 110-118.

513. Report on DeVisscher Paleo 2 Site—Also Some Illustrations of Recent Finds on Holcombe Site. The Totem Pole, Supplementary Bulletin. Aboriginal Research Club, Detroit, Mich., Oct., 1962. 2 unnumbered pages, 3 illus.

Article includes a drawing of a cross section of the DeVisscher Paleo 2 Site as well as an illustration of 11 artifacts discovered there. Also illustrates 11 other artifacts found at the Holcombe site.

514. Report on Northern Mississippi Area. American Antiquity, Vol. I, No. 3. The Society for American Archaeology, Menasha, Wis., 1936, pp. 229-230.

Report of archaeological activities and finds of the University of Michigan at Imlay City and in Lapeer County.

515. Reports from the Counties. Michigan History Magazine, Vol. II, No. 4, Whole No. 6. Michigan Historical Commission, Lansing, Oct., 1918, p. 673.

Tells of two mounds opened ca. 1874 in Ingham County and describes their contents.

516. Richards, Darrel, editor. The Ancient Copper Mines of Northern Michigan, Aboriginal Research Club, Detroit, Mich., n.d., pp. 112, illus.

A compilation from various sources of articles on ancient copper mining and the use of copper.

517. ——. The Galesburg Site, Vol. I, No. 1. Aboriginal Research Club, Detroit, Mich., n.d., pp. 3, 15 illus.

A report on the excavation of historic Indian graves by amateurs between 1895 and 1899.

518. ——. Pit Stones. The Totem Pole, Vol. II, No. 5. Aboriginal Research Club, Detroit, Mich., Feb., 1939, p. 5.

Reviews various theories for the probable use of pit stones.

519. ——. The Cranbrook Exhibit. The Totem Pole, Vol. III, No. 4. Aboriginal Research Club, Detroit, Mich., July, 1939, pp. 4-6, 1 illus.

Brief description of Michigan Indian artifacts then on display at the Cranbrook Institute of Science.

520. Richards, Darrel [J.]. Monroe County Sites. The Totem Pole, Vol. XL, No. 2. Aboriginal Research Club, Detroit, Mich., May, 1957, 3 unnumbered pp., 1 illus.

521. Richards, D[arrel J.]. More of Monroe County. The Totem Pole, Vol. XL, No. 3. Aboriginal Research Club, Detroit, Mich., June, 1957, 2 unnumbered pp.

522. Richards, Darrel J. The Petroglyphs. The Sanilac Petroglyphs, Bulletin XXXVI. Cranbrook Institute of Science, Bloomfield Hills, Mich., 1958, pp. 21-37, 16 illus.

See Petroglyphs — Index

523. ——. Fluted Points in Michigan. The Totem Pole, Vol. XLII, No. 3. Aboriginal Research Club, Detroit, Mich., March, 1959, 11 unnumbered pp., 7 illus.

524. R[ichards], D[arrel] J. [No title.] The Totem Pole, Vol. XLIII, No. 1. Aboriginal Research Club, Detroit, Mich., 1960, 2 unnumbered pp., 2 illus.

Locates and illustrates six artifacts found in Arenac County.

525. Richards, Darrel J. Paleo Points. The Totem Pole, Vol. XLV, No. 3. Aboriginal Research Club, Detroit, Mich., March, 1962, 6 unnumbered pp., 6 illus.

526. Rickard, T. A. The Use of Native Copper by the Indigenes of North America. The Journal of the Royal Anthropological Institute of Great Britain and Ireland, Vol. LXIV. Royal Anthropological Institute of Great Britain and Ireland, London, England, 1934, pp. 265-287, 3 illus.

527. Riley, Henry H. The Mound Builders and Their Work in Michigan. Michigan Pioneer and Historical Collections, Vol. III. Lansing, Mich., Robert Smith Printing Co., 1903, pp. 41-48.

528. Ringeisen, Jos., Jr. Birdstones of North America. The Wisconsin Archeologist, N.S., Vol. XI, No. 2. Wisconsin Archeological Society, Madison, Wis., Jan., 1932, pp. 33-40, 1 map.

Contains brief references to Michigan birdstones.

529. Ritzenthaler, Robert. Old Copper Specimens from Upper Michigan. The Wisconsin Archeologist, Vol. XXXIX, No. 2. Wisconsin Archeological Society, Milwaukee, Wis., June, 1958, pp. 151-152, 2 illus.

530. Rock Carvings. Michigan Archaeological Society News, Vol. II, No. 3. Michigan Archaeological Society, Ann Arbor, Aug., 1956, pp. 3-4.

Describes and gives the history of the rock carving in Sanilac County. See Petroglyphs — Index.

531. Rogers, Howard S. History of Cass County. Cassopolis, Mich., W. H. Mansfield, 1875, pp. 406.

Tells of garden beds and mounds in the county, pp. 49-51.

532. Roosa, William B. Michigan Fluted Point Sites. Michigan Archaeologist, Vol. VII, No. 2. Michigan Archaeological Society, Ann Arbor, June, 1961, pp. 11-12.

533. Root, William C. Metallurgical Examination of Five Copper Artifacts from Southern Michigan. *In* Griffin, James B., Editor. Lake Superior Copper and the Indians, Anthropological Papers, No. 17, Museum of Anthropology, University of Michigan. Ann Arbor, The University of Michigan, 1961, pp. 148-150.

534. Russell, John A. Prehistoric Discoveries in Wayne County, Michigan. Shelby Printing Co., Detroit, Mich., 1911, pp. 20.

Deals primarily with the Soper "finds." See Index.

535. ——. Notes on Prehistoric Discoveries in Wayne County, Michigan. The American Antiquarian and Oriental Journal, Vol. XXXIII, No. 3. Benton Harbor, Mich., The Antiquarian Publishing Co., July, Aug., Sept., 1911, pp. 135-143.

536. ——. Notes on Prehistoric Discoveries in Wayne County, Michigan. The American Antiquarian and Oriental Journal, Vol. XXXIII, No. 4. Benton Harbor, Mich., The Antiquarian Publishing Co., Oct., Nov., Dec., 1911, pp. 224-231.

## S

537. Sargent, H. E. Notes on the Mound Builder Monuments of Kent County, Michigan. Unpublished manuscript in the Grand Rapids Public Museum, Grand Rapids, Mich., April, 1915, pp. 12.

538. Savage, James. The Prehistoric Finds of Michigan. Records of the American Catholic Historical Society of Philadelphia, Vol. XXII, No. 1. American Catholic Historical Society, Philadelphia, Pa., March, 1911, pp. 21-38, 2 illus.

Includes data on the Soper "finds." See Index.

539. ——. Prehistoric Discoveries in Michigan. Shelby Printing Co., Detroit, Mich., 1911, pp. 16.

Reprint that reviews history of Lake Superior prehistoric copper mining and includes details of the discovery of the Soper "finds." Author participated in the uncovering of some of the latter.

540. Sawyer, Alvah L. A History of the Northern Peninsula of Michigan. Chicago, Lewis Publishing Co., 1911, pp. 272-273.

Gives details about the discovery of evidences of prehistoric mining of copper.

541. Schmidt, Walter L. Collecting Experiences in 1936: Shadow and Sunshine. The Totem Pole, Vol. XIII, No. 2. Aboriginal Research Club, Detroit, Mich., May, 1944, pp. 2-5, 1 illus.

Summary of surface finds made in and around Pinconning, Bay County, during 1936.

542. ——. A So-Called Sauk Mound Near Quanicasse, Michigan. The Totem Pole, Vol. XIX, No. 1. Aboriginal Research Club, Detroit, Mich., April, 1947, pp. 1-4.

543. ——. A Collecting Trip on the Potato River. The Totem Pole, Vol. XIX, No. 5. Aboriginal Research Club, Detroit, Mich., Aug., 1947, pp. 1-5.

Describes surface finds on the Potato River.

544. ——. Speculations of an Amateur Archaeologist. The Totem Pole, Vol. XXIV, No. 4. Aboriginal Research Club, Detroit, Mich., Jan., 1950, pp. 1-3.

545. ——. Arrow Points of Bay County, Michigan. The Totem Pole. Vol. XXVI, No. 3. Aboriginal Research Club, Detroit, Mich., Dec., 1950, pp. 1-4.

546. ——. Prehistoric Remains in Bay County, Michigan. The Totem Pole, Vol. XXX, No. 5. Aboriginal Research Club, Detroit, Mich., Feb., 1953, pp. 1-3.

547. ——. Bay County Chert Scrapers. The Totem Pole, Vol. XLI, No. 4. Aboriginal Research Club, Detroit, Mich., April, 1958, 3 unnumbered pp., 3 illus.

548. ——. Chert Drills from Bay County. The Totem Pole, Vol. XLI, No. 5. Aboriginal Research Club, Detroit, Mich., May, 1958, 3 unnumbered pp., 2 illus.

549. Schmidt, Walter, Sr. Where Do We Find Birdstones? The Totem Pole, Vol. XLII, No. 1. Aboriginal Research Club, Detroit, Mich., Jan., 1959, 14 unnumbered pp.,11 illus.

550. Schmidt, Walter, L. Birdstones of the Saginaw Bay Area. Michigan Archaeologist. Vol. VIII, No. 1. Michigan Archaeological Society, Ann Arbor, March, 1962, pp. 63-69, 3 illus.

551. Schneider, Robert. A Woodland Type Site at Hubbard Lake. The Totem Pole, Vol. X, No. 1. Aboriginal Research Club, Detroit, Mich., Oct., 1942, pp. 1-5, 3 illus.

552. Schoolcraft, Henry R. Historical and Statistical Information Respecting the History, Condition and Prospects of the Indian Tribes of the United States, Pt. I. Philadelphia, Lippincott, Grambo and Co., 1851.

553. ——. Information Respecting the History, Condition and Prospects of the Indian Tribes of the United States, 6 vols. Philadelphia, Lippincott, Grambo and Co., 1852-55, 1857.

See entry No. 448.

554. Science, N.S. [No title]. Vol. XV, No. 373. New York, The Macmillan Co., Feb., 1902, pp. 309-310.

A summary of a paper given by Harlan I. Smith on the Hauptman Earthwork in Ogemaw County.

555. Scotford, J. O. A Recent Mound Discovery by J. O. Scotford and Others. The American Archaeologist, Vol. II, Pt. 8. Columbus, O., The Landon Printing and Publishing Co., Aug., 1898, pp. 211-212.

A report of the discovery of the Soper "finds." See Index.

556. Setzler, Frank M. Archeological Perspectives in the Northern Mississippi Valley. Smithsonian Miscellaneous Collections, Vol. C, Publication 3588. Washington, D. C., Smithsonian Institution, May, 1940, pp. 253-287, 4 maps.

Author includes Michigan in his consideration of northern Mississippi Valley area archaeology.

557. Sheldon, W. H. Mounds in Michigan. American Antiquarian and Oriental Journal, Vol. IX, No. 6. Mendon, Ill., S. D. Peet, Nov., 1887, p. 365.

558. Sherzer, W. H. Geological Report on Wayne County. Michigan Geological and Biological Survey, Publication XII, Geological Series 9. Lansing, Mich., Wynkoop Hallenbeck Crawford Co., 1913, pp. 388.

Discusses Wayne County mounds and the Mound Builders.

559. Shetrone, Henry Clyde. The Mound-Builders. New York, D. Appleton & Co., 193, pp. 508.

560. Short, John T. The North Americans of Antiquity: Their Origin, Migrations and Type of Civilization Considered, 3d ed. New York, Harper & Brothers, 1882, pp. 29-30.

Contains a summation of mounds found in Michigan and the evidence of ancient copper mining in the northern part of the state.

561. A Site in Ingham County, Michigan. The Totem Pole, Vol. XLV, No. 4. Aboriginal Research Club, Detroit, Mich., April, 1962, 4 unnumbered pp., 2 illus.

562. Smith, Charles C. An Early Copper Enigma. Ohio Archaeologist, Vol. VII, No. 3. Dayton, Ohio, The Archaeological Society of Ohio, July, 1957, pp. 92-95, 3 illus.

Soper "finds" discussed and illustrated. See Index.

563. *Smith, Harlan I. Nests of Flint Implements in Michigan. American Antiquarian and Oriental Journal, Vol. XI, No. 4. Mendon, Ill., S. D. Peet, July, 1889, pp. 249-250.

564. ——. Primitive Remains in the Saginaw Valley, Michigan: The Ayres Mound. The Archaeologist, Vol. I, No. 3. Waterloo, Ind., March, 1893, pp. 51-53.

565. ——. Anthropological Work at the University of Michigan. Memoirs of the International Congress of Anthropology. Chicago, Ill., The Schulte Publishing Co., 1894, pp. 92-94.

566. ——. Anthropology at the University of Michigan. The University Record, Vol. III, No. 4. Ann Arbor, University of Michigan, Feb. 1894, pp. 98-100.

Contains a brief account of the beginnings of the study of anthropology at the University of Michigan. Also describes some of the archaeological materials at the University.

567. ——. Work in Anthropology at the University of Michigan for the Year 1892. Ann Arbor, The Courier Presses, 1894, pp. 14, 1 illus.

Reprint of above entry.

*See also*, Oakes, H. E., Pseud. for Harlan I. Smith, entry No. 449.

568. ——. Caches of the Saginaw Valley, Michigan. Proceedings of the American Association for the Advancement of Science, 42nd Meeting, Held at Madison, Wisconsin, August, 1893. Published by the Permanent Secretary, Salem, Mass., 1894, pp. 300-303, 2 illus.

569. ——. Archaeology of the Saginaw Valley. American Antiquarian and Oriental Journal, Vol. XVI, No. 2. Good Hope, Ill., Stephen D. Peet, March, 1894, pp. 106-109.

570. ——. Anthropologic Matters in Michigan. (Abstract.) Proceedings of the American Association for the Advancement of Science, 43rd Meeting Held at Brooklyn, New York, August, 1894. Published by the Permanent Secretary, Salem, Mass., 1895, pp. 352-353.

571. ——. The Development of Michigan Archaeology. Scientific American Supplement, Vol. XLII, No. 1084. New York, Munn & Co., Oct., 1896, pp. 17321-2.

572. ——. The Development of Michigan Archaeology. The Inlander, Vol. VI, No. 8. Published by the Students of the University of Michigan, Ann Arbor, May, 1896, pp. 307-310.

573. ——. Notes on the Data of Michigan Archaeology. The American Antiquarian and Oriental Journal, Vol. XVIII, No. 3, Pt. 1. Good Hope, Ill., Stephen D. Peet, May, 1896, pp. 144-153.

574. ——. Notes on the Data of Michigan Archaeology. Peoria, Ill., J. W. Franks and Son, 1896, pp. 9.

Reprint of above entry.

575. ——. Caches of the Saginaw Valley, Michigan. The Antiquarian, Vol. I, Pt. 2. Columbus, O., Landon Printing and Publishing Co., Feb., 1897, pp. 30-33, 2 illus.

576. ——. The Antiquities of Michigan, Their Value and Impending Loss. Detroit, Mich., John F. Eby and Co., 1901, pp. 12, 6 illus.

577. ——. Archeological Survey of Michigan. American Anthropologist, N.S., Vol. III, No. 1. New York, G. P. Putnam's Sons, Jan., 1901, pp. 198-200.

578. ——. Prehistoric Michigan. Popular Science, Vol. XXXV, No. 5. New York, Science News Company, May, 1901, pp. 110-111, 6 illus.

579. ——. Summary of the Archeology of Saginaw Valley, Michigan, Pt. I. American Anthropologist, N.S., Vol. III, No. 2. New York, G. P. Putnam's Sons, April-June, 1901, pp. 286-293.

580. ——. Summary of the Archeology of Saginaw Valley, Michigan, Pt. II. American Anthropologist, N.S., Vol. III, No. 3. New York, G. P. Putnam's Sons, July, 1901, pp. 501-512.

581. ——. Summary of the Archeology of Saginaw Valley, Michigan, Pt. III, American Anthropologist, N.S., Vol. III, No. 4. New York, G. P. Putnam's Sons, Oct., 1901, pp. 726-736.

582. ——. An Earthwork Discovered in Michigan. Science, N.S., Vol. XIII, No. 338. New York, The Macmillan Co., June, 1901, p. 991.

Report of a horseshoe-shaped earthwork in Ogemaw County.

583. ——. The Saginaw Valley Collection. Supplement to American Museum Journal, Vol. I, No. 12. American Museum of Natural History, New York, Nov.-Dec., 1901, pp. 1-24, 15 illus., 2 maps.

Material culture of Indians of Saginaw Valley as illustrated by objects on display at the American Museum of Natural History.

584. ——. The Antiquities of Michigan, Their Value and Impending Loss. Michigan Pioneer and Historical Collection, Vol. XXXI. Lansing, Mich., Wynkoop Hallenbeck Crawford Co., 1902, pp. 238-252, 6 illus.

See entry No. 576.

585. ——. An Archaeological Survey of Michigan. Third Report of the Michigan Academy of Science. Lansing, Mich., Wynkoop Hallenbeck Crawford Co., 1902, pp. 35-37.

586. ——. A Michigan Earth-Work and Its Impending Loss. American Antiquarian and Oriental Journal, Vol. XXVI, Chicago, S. D. Peet, March-April, 1904, pp. 121-122.

Threatened loss of Ogemaw County earthwork discussed.

587. ——. Preliminary List of the Sites of Aboriginal Remains in Michigan. Michigan Geological and Biological Survey, Publication I, Biological Series, No. 1. Lansing, Mich., Wynkoop Hallenbeck Crawford Co., 1910, pp. 67-89.

588. ——. Memoranda Towards a Bibliography of the Archaeology of Michigan. Michigan Geological and Biological Survey, Publication X, Biological Series, No. 3. Lansing, Mich., Wynkoop Hallenbeck Crawford Co., 1912, pp. 167-180.

589. ——. Field Notes. Unpublished manuscript in the Museum of Anthropology, University of Michigan, Ann Arbor.

590. Smith, Samuel Latta. Prehistoric and Modern Copper Mines of Lake Superior. Michigan Pioneer and Historical Collections, Vol. XXXIX. Lansing, Mich., Wynkoop Hallenbeck Crawford Co., 1915, pp. 137-151.

591. Some Wachtel Birds. Ohio Archaeologist, N.S., Vol. I, No. 1. Ohio Indian Relic Collectors Society, Columbus, April, 1951, p. 15, 1 illus.

Illustrates birdstones, two from Hillsdale County and one each from Ingham and Eaton Counties.

592. Spooner, H. L. The Big Mound at Springwells. Michigan History Magazine, Vol. XV, Summer No. Michigan Historical Commission, Lansing, 1931, pp. 446-453.

593. Spooner, A. L. Michigan's Controversial Finds. Aboriginal Research Club, Detroit, Mich., 1954, pp. 22, 2 illus.

A review of the Soper "finds." See Index.

594. ——. Those Controversial Michigan Tablets. Ohio Archaeologist, Vol. VII, No. 4. The Archaeological Society of Ohio, Dayton, Oct., 1957, pp. 131-132.

A response to the article under entry No. 562.

595. The Springwells Mound. The Totem Pole, Vol. XI, No. 4. Aboriginal Research Club, Detroit, Mich., July, 1943, p. 4.

A reprint of Henry Gillman's description of the mounds in Springwells Township, Wayne County. Original title or source not given.

596. A "Stamp" Tablet and Coin Found in a Michigan Mound. The American Antiquarian and Oriental Journal, Vol. XVI, No. 5. Good Hope, Ill., Stephen D. Peet, Sept., 1894, p. 313.

Refers to the Soper "finds." See Index.

597. Starr, Frederick. Perforated Skulls from Michigan. The American Antiquarian and Oriental Journal, Vol. XII, No. 3. Mendon, Ill., S. D. Peet, May, 1890, pp. 165-166.

598. Starr, Frederick, J. O. Kinnaman, and James E. Talmage. The Michigan Archaeological Question Settled. The American Antiquarian and Oriental Journal, Vol. XXXIII, No. 3. Benton Harbor, Mich., The Antiquarian Publishing Co., July, Aug., Sept., 1911, pp. 160-164.

599. Stephens, B. W. Forty Stephens Birdstones. Ohio Archaeologist, Vol. I, No. 2. Ohio Indian Relic Collectors Society, Columbus, July, 1951, p. 1, 1 illus.

600. Stevens, Edward J. Indian Trails, Mounds, Earthworks, Villages and Cemeteries in Kalamazoo County, Charles A. Weissert, editor. *In* Fuller, George N., Historic Michigan, Vol. III. Dayton, Ohio, National Historical Association, Inc., 1924, pp. 121-126.

601. ——. Michigan State Archeological Survey. Michigan History, Vol. XI, No. 3. Lansing, Michigan Historical Commission, July, 1927, pp. 436-444, 1 map.

602. ——. Topography and Prehistoric Cultures in Michigan. The Totem Pole, Vol. XXXIII, No. 3. Aboriginal Research Club, Algonac, Mich., Dec., 1953, pp. 1-4.

603. ——. Topography and Prehistoric Cultures in Michigan. The Totem Pole, Vol. XXXIII, No. 4. Aboriginal Research Club, Algonac, Mich., Jan., 1954, pp. 1-6.

604. Story of a Fort Near Muir, Michigan. The Archaeologist, Vol. I, No. 4. American Archaeological Assocation, Waterloo, Ind., April, 1893, pp. 65-67.

Describes Indian fort found in connection with the excavation of mounds at Muir. Reprinted from the Detroit News, Feb. 25, 1893.

605. Straw, Burton. Copper Mining Hammerstones from Upper Michigan. The Wisconsin Archeologist, N.S., Vol. XLIII, No. 3. Wisconsin Archeological Society, Milwaukee, Wis., Sept. 1962, p. 76, 1 illus.

606. Stroebel, Ralph W. A Cache of Chert Blades in Saginaw County, Michigan. American Antiquity, Vol. III, No. 2. Menasha, Wis., The Society for American Archaeology, 1937, pp. 186-187.

607. Summary of Correspondence. Annual Report, Smithsonian Institution, 1879. Washington, D. C., Government Printing Office, 1880, pp. 434-435.

Contains a summary of correspondence from nine individuals about Michigan archaeological sites and the contents of some.

608. Swineford, A. P. Annual Report of the Commissioner of Mineral Statistics of the State of Michigan for 1883. Marquette, Mich., Marquette Mining Journal Publishing House, 1884, pp. 117.

Contains a brief mention of prehistoric mining.

609. A System for Site Recording. Michigan Archaeological Society News, Vol. I, No. 4. Michigan Archaeological Society, Ann Arbor, Oct., 1954, pp. 5-7, 1 map.

Proposal of a system for recording the location of Michigan sites. See entry No. 42.

## T

610. Tatum, R. N. The Relation of Michigan Petroglyphs to Others in the United States. The Totem Pole, Vol. XVIII, No. 3. Aboriginal Research Club, Detroit, Mich., Dec., 1946, pp. 1-3.

611. Thomas, Cyrus. Catalogue of Prehistoric Works East of the Rocky Mountains. Bureau of American Ethnology, Bulletin No. 12, Smithsonian Institution. Washington, D. C., United States Government Printing Office, 1891, pp. 106-116, 1 map.

612. ——. Report on the Mound Explorations of the Bureau of Ethnology. 12th Annual Report, Bureau of American Ethnology, 1890-1891, Miscellaneous Documents, No. 82. Washington, D. C., Government Printing Office, 1894, pp. 516-519.

Rifle River and other mounds described. Also contains references to garden beds.

613. The Totem Pole, Vol. I, No. 5. Aboriginal Research Club, Detroit, Mich., Aug., 1938, 2 unnumbered pages.

A brief account of the contents of some 30 graves excavated on the Kalamazoo River, near Galesburg.

614. ——. Vol. XXXIX, No. 3. Aboriginal Research Club, Detroit, Mich., Dec., 1956, p. 7, 1 illus.

An axe found at Traverse City illustrated in full size.

615. Townsend, Earl C. Some Townsend Birds. Bulletin No. 26. Ohio Indian Relic Collectors Society, Columbus, Jan., 1951, p. 1, 1 illus.

Ten Michigan birdstones illustrated and identified by county of origin.

616. Townsend, Earl. Interesting Birds in the Townsend Collection. Ohio Archaeologist, N.S., Vol. I, No. 1. Ohio Indian Relic Collectors Society, Columbus, April, 1951, pp. 41-43, 1 illus.

617. Townsend, Earl C., Jr. Seventeen Birdstones from a Collection of 100 of Earl C. Townsend, Jr., Indianapolis. Ohio Archaeologist, N.S., Vol. III, No. 1. Ohio Indian Relic Collectors Society, Columbus, Jan., 1953, pp. 4-7, 1 illus.

618. ——. Twenty Birdstones from the Collection of Earl C. Townsend, Jr. Ohio Archaeologist, N.S., Vol. III, No. 2. Ohio Indian Relic Collectors Society, Columbus, April, 1953, pp. 6-8, 1 illus.

Four Michigan birdstones illustrated and identified by county of origin.

619. Birdstones of the North American Indian. (Privately published.) Indianapolis, Ind., 1959, p. 719.

Contains many references to Michigan birdstones.

620. The Traverse Region, Historical and Descriptive. Chicago, H. R. Page and Co., 1884, Chap. 1. "The Traverse Region," pp. 9-14.

Chapter includes "Traces of Mound Builders."

621. Troyer, Byron. The Boudeman Copper Collection. The Totem Pole, Vol. XXXV, No. 4. Aboriginal Research Club, Algonac, Mich., 1955, pp. 1-4, 1 illus.

622. Turner, Frank N., editor. Ingham County. *In* Fuller, George N., Historic Michigan, Vol. III, Dayton, Ohio, National Historical Association, Inc., 1924. Chap. I, "Introductory Review," pp. 17-44.

Chapter includes brief statements about and the location of Indian mounds in the county.

623. Two Copper Ornaments. The Totem Pole, Vol. XX, No. 2. Aboriginal Research Club, Detroit, Mich., Nov., 1947, pp. 1-2, 1 illus.

Outlines and describes the finding of two copper artifacts, one at Alpena and another at Escanaba.

## U

624. Ueck, Louis P. Material Used by the Southwest Michigan Indians in the Flaking of Stone Artifacts. The Earth Science Digest, Vol. VI, No. 6. Chicago, Ill., The Earth Science Publishing Company, May, 1953, pp. 31-33.

625. ——. A Fragmentary Projectile Point Cache. Michigan Archaeologist, Vol. VIII, No. 3. Michigan Archaeological Society, Ann Arbor, Sept., 1962, p. 27, 1 illus.

626. A Unique Find at Algonac. Michigan Archaeological Society News, Vol. I, No. 4. Michigan Archaeological Society, Ann Arbor, Oct., 1954, p. 8, 1 illus.

> Illustrates a hafted celt found in dredging the St. Clair River near Stag Island. Also tells of a 32-foot dugout recovered from Thousand Island Lake, Gogebic County.

627. University of Michigan Explorations. Michigan Archaeological Society News, Vol. I, No. 2. Michigan Archaeological Society, Ann Arbor, Jan., 1954, pp. 3-4.

> Briefly describes University of Michigan's search for archaeological sites in the Mackinac area; excavations on Keweenaw Point, and a visit to Isle Royale for charcoal samples.

## W

628. Wachtel, H. C. The Lowly Axe. Ohio Archaeologist, Vol. III, No. 4. Ohio Indian Relic Collectors Society, Columbus, Oct., 1953, pp. 22-23, 1 illus.

> Illustrates, describes and gives place of origin of some Michigan-type axes.

629. Wahla, Ed[ward] J. The Prehistoric Village Site at Huron City. The Totem Pole, Vol. XVI, No. 5. Aboriginal Research Club, Detroit, Mich., Feb., 1946, pp. 1-2, 1 map.

> Locates a village site near Huron City and describes surface features and surface finds.

630. ——. The Cass River. The Totem Pole, Vol. XXIII, No. 4. Aboriginal Research Club, Detroit, Mich., July, 1949, pp. 1-5.

> Refers to archaeological features and artifacts found on Cass River in 1834 as reported by W. R. McCormick in entry No. 421. Also gives details of current finds and collections of artifacts from the same region.

631. ——. An Owasco Burial Site in Oakland County, Michigan-Tessmer Site. The Totem Pole, Vol. XXVIII, No. 3. Aboriginal Research Club, Detroit, Mich., Dec., 1951, pp. 1-4.

632. ——. Two Ogemaw County Earthworks. The Totem Pole, Vol. XXXII, No. 3. Aboriginal Research Club, Detroit, Mich., June, 1953, pp. 3-4.

633. ——. (No title.) Chips from the Totem Pole, Aboriginal Research Club, Detroit, Mich., June, 1955, 1 p., 1 illus.

Report of the finding of a complete clay pot and an elbow pipe at the Swan Creek Site. Also tells of the discovery of a Hopewell knife blade at the Grand Rapids mounds in 1955. See entry No. 61.

634. ——, editor. (No title.) Chips from the Totem Pole. Aboriginal Research Club, Detroit, Mich., July, 1955, 1 p., 1 illus.

Gives details of the excavation of two burials in Chesterfield Township, north of Mount Clemens. Artifacts found of stone, copper and pottery, as well as human bone.

635. ——. (No title.) Chips from the Totem Pole. Aboriginal Research Club, Detroit, Mich., Oct., 1955, 1 p., 1 illus.

Brief description given of the excavation and the contents of a firepit in Chesterfield Township, near Riviere au Vase. Perforated skull, complete pottery vessel, elbow pipes, beads, etc., recovered. recovered.

636. ——. Observations on the Perforation and Cutting of Disks from Human Skulls. The Totem Pole, Vol. XXXVII, No. 4. Aboriginal Research Club, Detroit, Mich., Jan., 1956, 1 p.

637. ——. (No title.) Chips from the Totem Pole. Aboriginal Research Club, Detroit, Mich., [July?] 1956, 1 p.

Gives plans of members to engage in survey of Michigan earthworks. Some earthworks described.

638. ——. (No title.) Chips from the Totem Pole. Aboriginal Research Club, Detroit, Mich., Sept., 1956, 1 p.

Worked stone reported as found 60 feet from the Sanilac petroglyphs.

639. ——. (No title.) Chips from the Totem Pole, Aboriginal Research Club, Detroit, Mich., Dec., 1956, 1 p.

Tells of an Old Copper Culture burial found on the Tittabawassee River. Finds include human bones and copper artifacts.

640. ——. Some Prehistoric Michigan Pottery Pipes. The Totem Pole, Vol. XXXIX, No. 5. Aboriginal Research Club, Detroit, Mich., Feb., 1957, 2 unnumbered pp., 2 illus.

641. ——. (No title.) Chips from the Totem Pole. Aboriginal Research Club, Detroit, Mich., June, 1958, 1 p., 1 illus.

Report of artifacts, including pottery, found at a site in Clinton Township, Macomb County.

642. ——. (No title.) Chips from the Totem Pole. Aboriginal Research Club, Detroit, Mich., June, 1958, 1 p., 2 illus.

A rat-tail, tanged copper knife discovered in digging a well in Clinton Township, Macomb County.

643. ——. (No title.) Chips from the Totem Pole. Aboriginal Research Club, Detroit, Mich., Oct., 1958, 1 p.

Tells of burial site three miles north of St. Ignace consisting of 52 burials and contact materials.

644. ——. (No title.) Chips from the Totem Pole. Aboriginal Research Club, Detroit, Mich., Jan., 1959, 1 p., 1 illus.

Reports the finding of two stone axes near Emmet, one a Michigan-type barbed axe.

645. ——. (No title.) Chips from the Totem Pole. Aboriginal Research Club, Detroit, Mich., July, 1959, 1 p., 1 illus.

Fifty triangular unnotched points uncovered at Portage Site on Traverse Bay. Fire-cracked stones, flint flakes and spalls found in exploratory pits dug near the Sanilac petroglyphs.

646. ——. (No title.) Chips from the Totem Pole. Aboriginal Research Club, Detroit, Mich., Nov., 1959, 1 p., 1 illus.

Illustrates two fluted points or blades found in Cass Lake area, Oakland County, and Clinton Township, Macomb County.

647. ——. Michigan Barbed Axes. The Totem Pole, Vol. XLII, No. 9. Aboriginal Research Club, Detroit, Mich., Dec., 1959, 5 unnumbered pages, 3 illus.

648. ——. (No title.) Chips from the Totem Pole. Aboriginal Research Club, Detroit, Mich., March, 1960, 1 p., 1 illus.

Illustrates a gorget or amulet found in a pit at Riviere au Vase site.

649. ——. (No title.) Chips from the Totem Pole. Aboriginal Research Club, Detroit, Mich., Oct., 1960, 1 p., 1 illus.

Illustrates and describes the post-mold pattern of an Indian structure uncovered at the Moravian Delta Site, Clinton Township, Macomb County. Forty rim sherds found at same site.

650. ——. (No title.) Chips from the Totem Pole. Aboriginal Research Club, Detroit, Mich., Nov., 1960, 1 p., 1 illus.

Describes worked stone found on banks of Cass River in vicinity of Sanilac petroglyphs.

651. ——. (No title.) Chips from the Totem Pole. Aboriginal Research Club, Detroit, Mich., Jan., 1961, 1 p., 1 illus.

Illustrates and describes heretofore unreported artifacts found in a Hopewell Mound about 30 years ago in the Brooks Mound Group, Newaygo County.

652. ——. (No title.) Chips from the Totem Pole. Aboriginal Research Club, Detroit, Mich., Feb., 1961, 1 p., 1 illus.

Illustrates a slate birdstone, a two-holed slate gorget and a four-holed shell gorget, found in a Mackinaw City burial.

653. ——. (No title.) Chips from the Totem Pole. Aboriginal Research Club, Detroit, Mich., May, 1961, 1 p., 1 illus.

Tells of five Clovis-type points, a leaf-shaped artifact, five fluted butts, flakes, and spalls found at Paleo Site No. 2, Sterling Township, Macomb County.

654. ——. A Paleo-Indian Site in S. E. Michigan. The Coffinberry News Bulletin, Vol. VIII, No. 6. Wright L. Coffinberry Chapter, Michigan Archaeological Society, Grand Rapids, Mich., June, 1961, pp. 69-71, 1 illus.

655. ——. The Holcombe Paleo-Indian Site. The Totem Pole, Vol. XLIV, No. 7. Aboriginal Research Club, Detroit, Mich., Oct., 1961, 3 unnumbered pp., 1 illus.

656. ——. (No title.) Chips from the Totem Pole. Aboriginal Research Club, Detroit, Mich., Jan., 1962, 1 p., 1 illus.

Illustrates additional artifacts (12) found at Paleo Site No. 2, Sterling Township, Macomb County.

657. ——. (No title.) Chips from the Totem Pole. Aboriginal Research Club, Detroit, Mich., Feb., 1962, 1 p., 1 illus.

Notes a report by the Coffinberry Chapter, Michigan Archaeological Society, on its work at the Root Site, Delhi Township, Ingham County, in which bundle burials and some artifacts were uncovered.

658. ——. Scotts Bluff Aquaplano Sites in South Eastern Michigan. The Totem Pole, Vol. XLV, No. 2. Aboriginal Research Club, Detroit, Mich., Feb., 1962, 4 unnumbered pp., 2 illus., 1 map.

659. ——. (No title.) Chips from the Totem Pole. Aboriginal Research Club, Detroit, Mich., May, 1962, 1 p., 1 illus.

Further finds at Paleo Site No. 2, Sterling Township, Macomb County, described and illustrated.

660. ——. (No title.) Chips from the Totem Pole. Aboriginal Research Club, Detroit, Mich., Oct., 1962, 1 p., 1 illus.

Reports and illustrates a Michigan barbed axe found at Delaware Township, Sanilac County.

661. ——. Report on DeVisscher Paleo 2 Site. The Totem Pole. Supplementary Bulletin. Aboriginal Research Club, Detroit, Mich., Oct., 1962, 2 unnumbered pp., 2 illus.

662. ——. (No title.) Chips from the Totem Pole. Aboriginal Research Club, Detroit, Mich., Nov., 1962, 1 p., 1 illus.

Reports additional work done at Paleo Site No. 2, Sterling Township, Macomb County, and illustrates five recovered artifacts.

663. ——. Indian Wars of the Neutrals and the Michigan Fire Nation. The Totem Pole, Vol. XLV, No. 9. Aboriginal Research Club, Detroit, Mich., Dec., 1962, 11 unnumbered pp., 2 illus., 1 map.

Includes information on Neutral and other Indian sites and their contents.

664. Ward, Henry L. A Remarkable Ceremonial Object from Michigan. Bulletin of the Wisconsin Natural History Society, N.S., Vol. IV, No. 4. The Wisconsin Natural History Society, Milwaukee, Wis., 1906, pp. 160-161, 1 illus.

665. Weissert, Charles A. The Indians and the Trading Posts in the Northwest of Barry County, Michigan. Michigan Pioneer and Historical Collections, Vol. XXXVIII. Lansing, Mich., Wynkoop Hallenbeck Crawford Co., 1912, pp. 654-672.

666. Wells, David A. and George Bliss, Jr., editors. Geography and Antiquities: Ancient Mining Operations on Lake Superior. The Annual of Scientific Discovery: or Year-Book of Facts in Science and Art. Boston, Mass., Gould, Kendall and Lincoln, 1850, p. 360.

667. West, George A. The Indian Authorship of Wisconsin Antiquities. The Wisconsin Archeologist, [O.S.], Vol. VI, No. 4. Madison, Wis., Democrat Printing Co., Oct.-Dec., 1907, pp. 169-253, 11 illus.

Includes references to various Michigan mounds and to ancient Lake Superior copper mining.

668. ——. Copper: Its Mining and Use by the Aborigines of the Lake Superior Region. Bulletin of the Museum of the City of Milwaukee, Vol. X, No. 1. Public Museum of the City of Milwaukee, Milwaukee, Wis., May, 1929, pp. 182, 42 illus., 2 maps.

669. Whittlesey, Charles. The Ancient Miners of Lake Superior. The Canadian Journal, Vol. I, No. 5. Council of the Canadian Institute, Toronto, Dec., 1852, pp. 106-109.

670. ——. The Ancient Miners of Lake Superior. The Canadian Journal, Vol. I, No. 6. Council of the Canadian Institute, Toronto, Jan, 1853, pp. 132-135.

671. ——. The Ancient Miners of Lake Superior. The Annals of Science, Vol. I, No. 2. Cleveland, O., Harris and Fairbanks, 1853, pp. 15-18.

672. ——. The Ancient Miners of Lake Superior. The Annals of Science, Vol. I, No. 3. Cleveland, O., Harris and Fairbanks, 1853, pp. 27-30, 6 illus.

673. ——. On the Ancient Mining Operations of Lake Superior. (Abstract.) Proceedings of the American Association for the Advancement of Science, 11th Meeting, Held at Montreal, Canada, August 1857, Pt. II. Cambridge, Mass., Joseph Lovering, 1858, pp. 42-44.

674. ——. Ancient Mining on the Shores of Lake Superior. Smithsonian Contributions to Knowledge Vol. XIII, No. 155, Article 4. Washington, D. C., Smithsonian Institution, April, 1863, pp. 29, 21 illus., 1 map.

675. ——. On the Weapons and Military Character of the Race of the Mounds. Memoirs, Boston Society of Natural History, N.S., Vol. I, Pt. 4. Boston Society of Natural History, Boston, Mass., 1866-1869, pp. 475-481, 1 illus.

676. ——. The Ancient Miners of Lake Superior. *In* Drier, Roy Ward, and Octave Joseph Du Temple, editors. Prehistoric Copper Mining in the Lake Superior Region: A Collection of Reference Articles. Calumet, Mich., Drier and Du Temple, 1961, pp. 45-63.

677. Williams, Wolcott. The Past and Present of Eaton County, Michigan. Lansing, Mich., The Michigan Historical Publishing Association, N.D., pp. 12-13.

678. Wilson, Daniel. The Ancient Miners of Lake Superior. The Canadian Journal of Industry, Science and Art, N.S., Vol. I, No. 3. The Canadian Institute, Toronto, Canada, May, 1856, pp. 225-237, 1 illus.

679. Wilson, Thomas. Arrowpoints, Spearheads, and Knives of Prehistoric Times. Annual Report, United States National Museum, Smithsonian Institution, 1897, Pt. 1. Washington, D. C., Government Printing Office, 1899, pp. 811-1021.

Gives locations and contents of caches of arrow and spear points found in Saginaw Valley on p. 980.

680. Winchell, N. H. The Geological and Natural History Survey of Minnesota. The Ninth Annual Report, for the Year 1880. St. Peter, Minn., J. K. Moore, 1881, pp. 162-164.

Lists hammerstones, charred wood and pounded copper flakes found on Isle Royale.

681. ——. Ancient Copper Mines of Isle Royale. The Popular Science Monthly, Vol. XIX. New York, Appleton & Co., Sept., 1881, pp. 601-620, 8 illus.

682. ——. Ancient Copper Mines of Isle Royale. The Engineering and Mining Journal, Vol. XXXII, No. 12. New York, The Scientific Publishing Company, Sept. 17, 1881, pp. 184-186, 8 illus.

683. ——. Ancient Copper Mines of Isle Royale. The Engineering and Mining Journal, Vol. XXXII, No. 13. New York, The Scientific Publishing Co., Sept. 24, 1881, pp. 201-202.

Reprint of entry No. 681.

684. ——. Ancient Copper Mines of Isle Royale. *In* Drier, Roy Ward, and Octave Joseph Du Temple, editors. Prehistoric Copper Mining in the Lake Superior Region: A Collection of Reference Articles. Calumet, Mich., Drier and Du Temple, 1961, pp. 103-115.

Same as entry No. 681.

685. Witherall, Benjamin F. H. Mounds of the Dead, on Springwells Sand Hill. (Extract.) *In* Address of President John C. Holmes, at the Annual Meeting of June 7, 1882. Michigan Pioneer and Historical Collections, Vol. V. Lansing, Mich., Robert Smith Printing Co., 1904, pp. 4-6.

686. The Woodland Pattern. Michigan Archaeological Society News, Vol. II, No. 3. Michigan Archaeological Society, Ann Arbor, Aug., 1956, pp. 4-7.

Gives the trait list of the Woodland Pattern.

687. Writer's Program of the Work Projects Administration in the State of Michigan. Michigan: A Guide to the Wolverine State. American Guide Series. New York, Oxford University Press, 1946, pp. 682.

Tells of mounds, enclosures, garden beds, villages, cemeteries, mines, etc., in Michigan.

688. Wyman, Jeffries. Indian Mounds and Skulls in Michigan. Results of Explorations of Mr. Henry Gillman. American Journal of Science and Arts, Vol. VII, Whole Number CVII, 3d Ser., No. 37-42. New Haven, Conn., Tuttle, Morehouse and Taylor, Jan. to June, 1874, pp. 1-9.

## Y

689. Yaggie, Ida. An Early Trade Hatchet. Ohio Archaeologist, Vol. VIII, No. 2. The Archaeological Society of Ohio, Columbus, April, 1958, p. 65, 1 illus.

Illustrates and describes an iron hatchet found at Mackinaw [City?]

690. Yesterday's with the Magazine: Prehistoric Indian Lore. Michigan History, Vol. XXV, Winter No., Michigan Historical Commission, Lansing, Mich., 1941, pp. 100-101, 104-107, 2 illus., 1 map.

Includes a group photograph of the personnel of the Franklin Isle Royale expedition of 1923 (pp. 100-101); map of garden beds and text regarding their probable origin and use (pp. 104-105); some arrow points in the collection of the Michigan Historical Commission Museum (pp. 106-107).

691. Young, T. Hugh. Birdstones. Ohio Archaeologist, Vol. V, No. 3. The Archaeological Society of Ohio, Columbus, July, 1955, pp. 92-93, 1 illus.

Four Michigan birdstones illustrated.

692. ——. Birdstones. Ohio Archaeologist, Vol. V, No. 4. The Archaeological Society of Ohio, Columbus, Oct., 1955, pp. 134-135, 1 illus.

Illustrates two birdstones from Michigan.

## Z

693. Zakucia, John A. The Birdstone, An Enigma of the Prehistoric Past. Ohio Archaeologist, N.S., Vol. I, No. 2. Ohio Indian Relic Collectors Society, Columbus, July, 1951, pp. 35-36, 1 illus.

Illustrates and gives county of origin of ten Michigan birdstones.

# ADDENDA

## A

1. Archeologists Flock to Employee's Farm to Study Ancient Indian Burial Grounds Found by Workers. Michigan General News, Vol. IV, No. 10. General Telephone Company of Michigan, Muskegon, May 1963, p. 4, 1 illus.

See Addenda entries Nos. 50 and 52.

## B

2. Binford, Lewis R., and Mark L. Papworth. The Eastport Site, Antrim County, Michigan. *In* Miscellaneous Studies in Typology and Classification, Anthropological Papers, Museum of Anthropology, University of Michigan, No. 19. University of Michigan, Ann Arbor, 1963, pp. 71-123, 9 illus., 11 tab.

3. Binford, Lewis R. The Hodges Site. A Late Archaic Burial Station. *In* Miscellaneous Studies in Typology and Classification, Anthropological Papers, Museum of Anthropology, University of Michigan, No. 19. University of Michigan, Ann Arbor, 1963, pp. 124-148, 3 illus., 7 tab.

4. ______. The Pomranky Site. A Late Archaic Burial Station. *In* Miscellaneous Studies in Typology and Classification, Anthropological Papers, Museum of Anthropology, University of Michigan, No. 19. University of Michigan, Ann Arbor, 1963, pp. 149-192, 6 illus., 13 tab.

5. ______. An Analysis of Cremations from Three Michigan Sites. The Wisconsin Archeologist, N. S., Vol. XLIV, No. 2. The Wisconsin Archeological Society, Milwaukee, June, 1963, pp. 98-110, 2 tab.

6. Black, Meredith, and Charles E. Eyman. The Union Lake Skull, A Possible Early Indian Find in Michigan. American Antiquity, Vol. XXIX, No. 1. Society for American Archaeology, Salt Lake City, Utah, July, 1963, pp. 39-48, 2 illus.

Human skull found in Oakland County peat deposit. May be from 5,000 B. C.

## C

7. Cleland, Charles E. A Late Archaic Burial from Washtenaw County, Michigan. Michigan Archaeologist, Vol. IX, No. 3. Michigan Archaeological Society, Ann Arbor, Oct. 1963, pp. 41-44, 1 illus.

8. Coffinberry, Wright L. Coffinberry Manuscript—Article VI. The Coffinberry News Bulletin, Vol. X, No. 1. Wright L. Coffinberry Chapter, Michigan Archaeological Society, Grand Rapids, Jan. 1963, pp. 4-6.

See entries Nos. 58 and 59.

9. ______. Coffinberry Manuscript—Article VII. The Coffinberry News Bulletin, Vol. X, No. 2. Wright L. Coffinberry Chapter, Michigan Archaeological Society, Grand Rapids, Feb., 1963, pp. 18-20.

10. ______. Coffinberry Manuscript—Article VII. The Coffinberry News Bulletin, Vol. X, No. 3. Wright L. Coffinberry Chapter, Michigan Archaeological Society, Grand Rapids, March, 1963, pp. 22-26.

11. ______. Coffinberry Manuscript—Article VII. The Coffinberry News Bulletin, Vol. X, No. 4. Wright L. Coffinberry Chapter, Michigan Archaeological Society, Grand Rapids, April, 1963, pp. 34-35.

12. ______. Coffinberry Manuscript, Conclusion to Article VII. The Coffinberry News Bulletin, Vol. X, No. 5. Wright L. Coffinberry Chapter, Michigan Archaeological Society, Grand Rapids, May, 1963, pp. 46-47.

13. ______. The Coffinberry Manuscript, Article VIII. The Coffinberry News Bulletin, Vol. X, No. 6. Wright L. Coffinberry Chapter, Michigan Archaeological Society, Grand Rapids, June, 1963, pp. 55-56.

14. ______. The Coffinberry Manuscript, Starting—Article No. 9. The Coffinberry News Bulletin, Vol. X, No. 8. Wright L. Coffinberry Chapter, Michigan Archaeological Society, Grand Rapids, Sept., 1963, pp. 85-86.

15. ______. Coffinberry Manuscript, Continuing Article No. 9. The Coffinberry News Bulletin, Vol. X, No. 9. Wright L. Coffinberry Chapter, Michigan Archaeological Society, Grand Rapids, Oct., 1963, pp. 95-97.

16. ______. Coffinberry Manuscript, Article 10. The Coffinberry News Bulletin, Vol. X, No. 10. Wright L. Coffinberry Chapter, Michigan Archaeological Society, Grand Rapids, Nov., 1963, pp. 103-106.

17. ______. Coffinberry Manuscript (Article No. 10, Continued from November). The Coffinberry News Bulletin, Vol. X, No. 11. Wright L. Coffinberry Chapter, Michigan Archaeological Society, Grand Rapids, Dec., 1963, pp. 113-114.

18. Cornelius, Eldon S. Porter Site 1, Midland County, Michigan. The Totem Pole, Vol. XLVI, No. 2. Aboriginal Research Club, Detroit, Mich., Feb., 1963, pp. 3, 3 illus.

19. ______. Porter Site 13. The Totem Pole, Vol. XLVI, No. 7. Aboriginal Research Club, Detroit, Mich., Oct., 1963, pp. 60-62, 3 illus.

20. ______. Porter Site 15. The Totem Pole, Vol. XLVI, No. 8. Aboriginal Research Club, Detroit, Mich., Nov., 1963, p. 68, 1 illus.

21. Cunningham, W. M. Porphyry Pop-Eye Bird. Ohio Archaeologist, Vol. 13, No. 1. The Archaeological Society of Ohio, Columbus, Jan., 1963, p. 21, 1 illus.

Illustrates and describes a birdstone found in Berrien County in 1925.

D

22. Davis, George W. W. L. C. Hosts M. A. S. Workshop Conf. The Coffinberry News Bulletin, Vol. X, No. 7. Wright L. Coffinberry Chapter, Michigan Archaeological Society, Grand Rapids, July-Aug., 1963, pp. 70-73.

23. De Visscher, Jerry. Surface Finds on Various Parts of the Holcombe Site Beach. The Totem Pole, Vol. XLVI, No. 5. Aboriginal Research Club, Detroit, Mich., May, 1963, pp. 37-38, 1 illus.

24. The De Visscher Paleo II Occupation Site. The Totem Pole, Vol. XLVI, No. 6. Aboriginal Research Club, Detroit, Mich., June, 1963, pp. 44-56, 7 illus.

25. Doty, Tom. Some Montcalm County Finds. The Totem Pole, Vol. XLVI, No. 5. Aboriginal Research Club, Detroit, Mich., May, 1963, p. 40, 1 illus.

E

26. Emmert, Darlene Gay. The Indians of Shiawassee County. Michigan History, Vol. XLVII, No. 2. Michigan Historical Commission, Lansing, June, 1963, pp. 127-155, 1 map.

Includes brief archaeological data and a map of Shiawassee County sites. See entry No. 27, below.

27. ______. The Indians of Shiawassee County. Michigan History, Vol. XLVII, No. 3. Michigan Historical Commission, Lansing, Sept., 1963, pp. 243-272.

F

28. Fish, Paul. Beaver Mound, Lenawee County, Michigan. Ohio Archaeologist, Vol. XIII, No. 1. The Archaeological Society of Ohio, Columbus, Jan., 1963, p. 29.

Describes and locates an unexcavated beaver effigy mound.

29. Fitting, James E. Thickness and Fluting of Paleo-Indian Projectile Points. American Antiquity, Vol. XXIX, No. 1. The Society for American Archaeology, Salt Lake City, Utah, July, 1963, pp. 105-106.

30. ______. The Hi-Lo Site: A Progress Report. The Coffinberry News Bulletin, Vol. X, No. 6. Wright L. Coffinberry Chapter, Michigan Archaeological Society, Grand Rapids, June, 1963, pp. 57-58.

Formerly called Flat River Site. See entry No. 215.

31. ______. An Early Post Fluted Point Tradition in Michigan: A Distributional Analysis. Michigan Archaeologist, Vol. IX, No. 2. Michigan Archaeological Society, Ann Arbor, July, 1963, pp. 21-24, 1 illus.

32. ______. The Welti Site: A Multi-Component Site in Southeastern Michigan. Michigan Archaeologist, Vol. IX, No. 3. Michigan Archaeological Society, Ann Arbor, Oct., 1963, pp. 34-40, 3 illus., 1 tab.

33. ______. The Hi-Lo Site, A Late Paleo-Indian Site in Western Michigan. The Wisconsin Archeologist, N. S., Vol. XLIV, No. 2. The Wisconsin Archeological Society, Milwaukee, June, 1963, pp. 87-96, 3 illus., 1 tab.

34. Flanders, Richard E. Marion Thick Pottery in Michigan. The Coffinberry News Bulletin, Vol. X, No. 5. Wright L. Coffinberry Chapter, Michigan Archaeological Society, Grand Rapids, May, 1963, pp. 47-48.

35. Fogel, Ira L. The Dispersal of Copper Artifacts in the Late Archaic Period of Prehistoric North America. The Wisconsin Archeologist, N. S., Vol. XLIV, No. 3. The Wisconsin Archeological Society, Milwaukee, Sept., 1963, pp. 129-180, 4 illus., 15 tab., 14 maps.

36. Fox, Geo. Indian Earthworks, Burials and Mounds in Cass County, Michigan. The Totem Pole, Vol. XLVI, No. 1. Aboriginal Research Club, Detroit, Mich., Jan., 1963, pp. 3.

37. Frankforter, W. D. How Chapter Members Can Participate. The Coffinberry News Bulletin, Vol. X, No. 6. Wright L. Coffinberry Chapter, Michigan Archaeological Society, Grand Rapids, June, 1963, pp. 61-63.

Tells how chapter members can help in the excavation of the Norton Mounds and gives the history of events leading to the project. See Addenda entry No. 46.

38. ______. The Norton Mound Project. The Coffinberry News Bulletin, Vol. X, No. 7. Wright L. Coffinberry Chapter, Michigan Archaeological Society, Grand Rapids, July-Aug., 1963, pp. 66-68.

39. Franz, Harvey, editor. News Letter, Vol. X, No. 8. Southwest Chapter, Michigan Archeological Society, Benton Harbor, Jan., 1963, pp. 2.

Quotes a newspaper report on the opening of mounds in the region of Berrien Springs, Michigan, by railroad builders. Also quotes 1888 newspaper report on the excavation of 15 Sumnerville mounds by E. H. Crane. Contents of both mound groups noted.

40. ______. News Letter, Vol. X, No. 9. Southwest Chapter, Michigan Archeological Society, Benton Harbor, Feb., 1963, p. 1.

Quotes newspaper reports of a fort and several mounds and their contents, near Sumnerville.

41. ______. News Letter, Vol. XI, No. 1. Southwest Chapter, Michigan Archeological Society, Benton Harbor, May, 1963, p. 2.

Contains brief mention of skeletal material found in various parts of the state.

42. ______. News Letter, Vol. XI, No. 2. Southwest Chapter, Michigan Archeological Society, Benton Harbor, June, 1963, pp. 1 and 2, 1 illus.

Mentions artifacts found in various parts of the state during 1963. Illustrates a six and one-half inch flint spear point found in Benton Township.

43. ______. News Letter, Vol. XI, No. 6. Southwest Chapter, Michigan Archeological Society, Benton Harbor, Oct., 1963, pp. 2.

Reports the discovery of 144 blades on the west side of St. Joseph River. See Addenda entry No. 64.

G

44. Gillis, E. V. A Marion Thick Pottery Find at Grand Rapids, Mich. The Coffinberry News Bulletin, Vol. X, No. 5. Wright L. Coffinberry Chapter, Michigan Archaeological Society, Grand Rapids, May, 1963, pp. 48-50, 1 illus.

45. [Gillis, E. V., editor.] A Loop-Handle Rim Sherd. The Coffinberry News Bulletin, Vol. X, No. 6, Wright L. Coffinberry Chapter, Michigan Archaeological Society, Grand Rapids, June, 1963. pp. 58-59, 1 illus.

46. Gillis, E. V. W. L. Coffinberry Chapter's Contribution to the Development of Indian Mound Park (Norton Mound Site). The Coffinberry News Bulletin, Vol. X, No. 6. Wright L. Coffinberry Chapter, Michigan Archaeological Society, Grand Rapids, June, 1963, pp. 59-61.

See Addenda entry No. 37.

47. [Gillis, E. V., editor.] Some News on Progress of Norton Mounds Report. The Coffinberry News Bulletin, Vol. X, No. 11, Wright L. Coffinberry Chapter, Michigan Archaeological Society, Grand Rapids, Dec., 1963, pp. 110-111.

48. Green, Amos R. The Prillwitz Mammoth. The Coffinberry News Bulletin, Vol. X, No. 2. Wright L. Coffinberry Chapter, Michigan Archaeological Society, Grand Rapids, Feb., 1963, pp. 15-18.

Gives details of the discovery of mammoth bones and Clovis type points found in Berrien County. See Addenda entry No. 65.

49. ______. The Prillwitz Mammoth, Part II. The Coffinberry News Bulletin, Vol. X, No. 3. Wright L. Coffinberry Chapter, Michigan Archaeological Society, Grand Rapids, March, 1963, pp. 28-29, 1 illus.

See Addenda entry No. 65.

50. [Griffin, Leonard, editor.] Field Season Begins for Clinton Valley. Arti-facts, Vol. I, No. 5. Clinton Valley Chapter, Michigan Archaeological Society, June, 1963, pp. 1-2.

Brief mention of salvage operation and finds at a Capac, Michigan burial site by Clinton Valley Chapter and University of Michigan. See Addenda entry No. 52.

51. Griffin, Leonard. A Handbook for the Amateur Archaeologist. Division of Continuing Education, Oakland University, Rochester, Mich., rev. ed., 1963, pp. 84, 6 illus.

52. Hagge, Donald. Continuing Study of the Hunter Site Near Capac, Michigan. Arti-Facts, Vol. II, No. 1. Clinton Valley Chapter, Michigan Archaeological Society, Nov., 1963, pp. 4-5.

See Addenda entry No. 50.

H

53. Hays, Donald R. Notes and Abstracts of Papers of the Annual Meeting in East Lansing on April 28, 1963. Michigan Archaeologist, Vol. IX, No. 2. Michigan Archaeological Society, Ann Arbor, July, 1963, pp. 14-16.

54. Hill, Clarence. A Sanilac County Site. The Totem Pole, Vol. XLVI, No. 8. Aboriginal Research Club, Detroit, Mich., Nov., 1963, p. 67, 1 illus.

J

55. A Jackson County, Michigan Site. The Totem Pole, Vol. XLVI, No. 8. Aboriginal Research Club, Detroit, Mich., Nov., 1963, pp. 69-70, 2 illus.

L

56. Laut, Jack. A Workshop Site in Oakland County, Michigan. The Totem Pole, Vol. XLVI, No. 9. Aboriginal Research Club, Detroit, Mich., Dec., 1963, p. 73, 5 illus.

M

57. McPherron, Alan L. . Late Woodland Ceramics in the Straits of Mackinac. Michigan Academy of Science, Arts, and Letters, Vol. XLVIII. The University of Michigan Press, Ann Arbor, 1963, pp. 567-576, 3 illus.

58. Memorial. Michigan Archaeologist, Vol. IX, No. 2. Michigan Archaeological Society, Ann Arbor, July, 1963, pp. 25-28.

A memorial to the late George R. Fox, including a bibliography of his archaeological writings.

P

59. Peske, G. Richard. Argillite of Michigan: A Preliminary Projectile Point Classification and Temporal Placement from Surface Materials. Michigan Academy of Science, Arts, and Letters, Vol. XLVIII. The University of Michigan Press, Ann Arbor, 1963, pp. 557-566, 1 illus., 1 map.

60. Petersen, Eugene T. Some 18th Century Clay Pipes Found at Mackinac. Michigan Archaeologist, Vol. IX, No. 1. Michigan Archaeological Society, Ann Arbor, March,1963, pp. 1-6, 5 illus.

Q

61. Quimby, George I. A New Look at Geochronology in the Upper Great Lakes Region. American Antiquity, Vol. XXVIII, No. 4. Society for American Archaeology, Salt Lake City, Utah, April, 1963, pp. 558-559.

62. ______. Late Period Copper Artifacts in the Upper Great Lakes Region. The Wisconsin Archeologist, Vol. XLIV, No. 4, The Wisconsin Archeological Society, Milwaukee, Dec., 1963, pp. 193-198, 2 illus.

R

63. Roosa, William B. Some Michigan Fluted Point Sites and Types. Michigan Archaeologist, Vol. IX, No. 3. Michigan Archaeological Society, Ann Arbor, Oct., 1963, pp. 44-48, 2 illus.

U

64. Ueck, Louis P. A Report on a Discovery of Cache Blades in Berrien County, Michigan. Michigan Archaeologist, Vol. IX, No. 2. Michigan

Archaeological Society, Ann Arbor, July, 1963, p. 20,1 illus.

See Addenda entry No. 43.

W

65. Wahla, Ed [ward] J., editor. Chips from the Totem Pole. Aboriginal Research Club, Detroit, Mich., April, 1963, p. 1.

Brief mention of mammoth bones found in Berrien County. See Addenda entries Nos. 48 and 49.

66. ______. Chips from the Totem Pole. Aboriginal Research Club, Detroit, Mich., Nov., 1963, p. 1, 1 illus.

Reports and illustrates a small castellated pot found at a Wayne County site.

67. ______. Tessmer Prehistoric Cemetery, Oakland County. Michigan Archaeologist, Vol. IX, No. 1. Michigan Archaeological Society, Ann Arbor, March, 1963, pp. 7-11.

68. ______. Rare Find. The Totem Pole, Vol. XLVI, No. 5. Aboriginal Research Club, Detroit, Mich., May, 1963, p. 41, 1 illus.

Illustrates,in full size, a Hopewell pot and an arrow point found in a mound near Nunica.

69. Woolworth, Alan R. and Nancy L. Thirty Old Copper Culture Artifacts from Michigan. Michigan Archaeologist, Vol. IX, No. 2. Michigan Archaeological Society, Ann Arbor, July, 1963, pp. 17-19, 1 map.

# INDEX

(By entry number)*



*Addenda entries not included in Index.

G



H



I



M



O



P



R



S

www.ingramcontent.com/pod-product-compliance
Lightning Source LLC
LaVergne TN
LVHW050022250826
846302LV00008B/63
*9781949098235*